THE VIRGIN
MOVIE QUIZ
BOOK

THE VIRGIN
MOVIE QUIZ
BOOK

Alan Ferguson

First published in Great Britain in 2004 by
Virgin Books Ltd
Thames Wharf Studios
Rainville Road
London
W6 9HA

Copyright © Alan Ferguson 2004

The right of Alan Ferguson to be identified as the
Author of this Work has been asserted by him in
accordance with the Copyright, Designs and
Patents Act, 1998.

A catalogue record for this book is available from
the British Library.

ISBN 0 7535 0829 X

Designed by Undertow
Typeset by Phoenix Photosetting, Chatham, Kent
Printed and bound in Great Britain by Clays Ltd,
St Ives PLC

To
Paola, Federico and Giorgia

CONTENTS

BACKGROUND

Everyone who loves movies always remembers their first visit to the cinema and subsequently the first film they ever saw on the big screen. Everyone except me, that is! That particular childhood memory that should have stayed with me forever, instead became an instantly forgettable one.

It's not difficult to imagine which classic film it might have been – *The Sound of Music, Mary Poppins, Oliver!* or *Chitty Chitty Bang Bang*. They were all classic children's films from a decade in which, as a small child, I would often visit the local 'picture house' with my mother and father.

The first film I truly remember seeing in the cinema was the 1973 James Bond film, *Live and Let Die*. Unfortunately, this was more for the recollection of receiving the glossy booklet about the film that was on sale in the foyer!

It wasn't until maybe a year later that I went to see a wonderful 'cops and robbers' type action film, which I believe to be the start of my love affair with Hollywood. My father was understandably a little reluctant to be dragged along to see a film which he believed to be just a little too 'grown-up' for his impressionable son. It probably only seemed like yesterday to him that I was happy enough to munch my way through a bucket of popcorn while watching *The Aristocats* or some other equally inoffensive film. Only now can I understand his apprehension about the sudden leap from cartoon cats and the safe, fluffy world of Walt Disney, to the harsh reality of such adult fare, but things were a little different at the time.

After many days of the 'Oh, pleeeese, Dad' type of manipulation, my father finally succumbed to the pressure of a very persuasive twelve-year-old kid. And so it was that one Saturday afternoon in 1974 changed my life.

What was the name of that film?

It was the Robert Shaw/Walter Matthau thriller, *The Taking of Pelham 123*. The story was simple enough: a gang of thieves hijack a New York City subway train and hold the passengers to ransom. Robert Shaw was the leader of the gang and Walter Matthau was the grisly old transit cop on his trail – and I thought it was all just so wonderfully exciting.

It wasn't until a long, long time afterwards that I finally stopped talking about how good a film it was.

The rest, as they say, is history. From that moment on I was hooked on the wonderful world of Hollywood and this little book is the result.

It only remains for me to say a big thank you to my father and of course to the makers of that fabulous film.

FOREGROUND

All the questions are based on the Hollywood movies released during the last 25 years (1978–2003). Only chapters 30 and 34 (for obvious reasons) include themes from before this period.

The 1,500 big, beautiful questions over which to ponder, deliberate and contemplate are sprawled over 40 chapters, 66 sub-chapters and lots and lots of pages! The answers, on the other hand, are squashed into a few pages at the back somewhere!

Enjoy!

SCORECARD

If you really must measure the exact extent of your movie knowledge, award yourself a point for each correct answer and use the scorecard below to keep a note of your progress (or lack of) through the chapters.

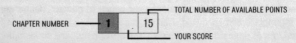

CHAPTER NUMBER → **1** [ ] **15** ← TOTAL NUMBER OF AVAILABLE POINTS
← YOUR SCORE

YOUR SCORES										
1		15	**9**		60	**17**		36	**25**		25	**33**		40
2		30	**10**		100	**18**		30	**26**		20	**34**		61
3		30	**11**		40	**19**		20	**27**		32	**35**		48
4		76	**12**		31	**20**		30	**28**		20	**36**		30
5		30	**13**		50	**21**		50	**29**		60	**37**		30
6		20	**14**		30	**22**		30	**30**		26	**38**		40
7		40	**15**		14	**23**		80	**31**		30	**39**		15
8		45	**16**		10	**24**		77	**32**		48	**40**		1
TOTAL		1500												

And what it all means . . .

< 50	Just how stupid are you?
50–199	Maybe you should try a sports quiz!
200–499	Not bad, but not very good either!
500–999	Mr/s Average
1000–1299	Impressive!
1300–1400	Genius or cheat. Which is it?
> 1400	Get a life!

QUESTIONS

1 TOO EASY

To help get you started . . .

1 Sex, lies and what else?
2 How many weddings and how many funerals?
3 Who played the part of Indiana Jones?
4 Who directed *ET: The Extra-Terrestrial* (1982)?
5 What was Frodo Baggins?
6 Who was the dog? Turner or Hooch?
7 Which famous basketball player saved Bugs, Daffy and the rest of the Looney Tunes from alien invaders in 1996?
8 What were the names of those two annoying little robots ever-present in *Star Wars* (1977–2005)?
9 How many times did Marty McFly go back to the future?
10 What was Michael Corleone better known as?
11 Who played the part of 'Shorty' in *Get Shorty* (1995)?
12 Who was the 'next generation' captain of the USS Enterprise?
13 In which series of films did Bruce Willis play an N.Y.P.D. cop called John McClane?
14 Who stayed home alone while the rest of the family enjoyed their Christmas vacation in Paris?
15 What was Stuart Little?

? **2 THE NAME GAME**

Who played the title role(s) in the following films?

1 *Mr Saturday Night* (1992)
2 *Johnny Mnemonic* (1995)
3 *Mrs Soffel* (1984)
4 *Jerry and Tom* (1998)
5 *Bronco Billy* (1980)
6 *Doc Hollywood* (1991)
7 *Captain Ron* (1992)
8 *V.I. Warshawski* (1991)
9 *Nell* (1994)
10 *John Q* (2002)
11 *Nadine* (1987)
12 *Mr Deeds* (2002)
13 *Barton Fink* (1991)
14 *Mad Dog and Glory* (1993)
15 *Tom Horn* (1980)

16 *Me, Myself & Irene* (2000)
17 *Agatha* (1979)
18 *Jack* (1996)
19 *Dolores Claiborne* (1995)
20 *G.I. Jane* (1997)
21 *Frankie and Johnny* (1991)
22 *Edward Scissorhands* (1990)
23 *Erin Brockovich* (2000)
24 *Mr Jones* (1993)
25 *Oscar and Lucinda* (1997)
26 *Blaze* (1989)
27 *Ethan Frome* (1993)
28 *Frida* (2002)
29 *Mr & Mrs Bridge* (1990)
30 *Hannah and Her Sisters* (1986)

3 WHODUNNIT

1 Who had a *One Night Stand* (1997)?
2 Who fell *Overboard* (1987)?
3 Who built a *Field of Dreams* (1989)?
4 Who was *Guilty by Suspicion* (1991)?
5 Who worked the *Night Shift* (1982)?
6 Who found a *Message in a Bottle* (1999)?
7 Who showed *Courage Under Fire* (1996)?
8 Who wanted to *Throw Momma from the Train* (1987)?
9 Who had *Nowhere to Run* (1993)?
10 Who wanted *Proof of Life* (2000)?
11 Who made *Contact* (1997)?
12 Who was *Married to the Mob* (1988)?
13 Who was photographing *The Bridges of Madison County* (1995)?
14 Who did things *The Hard Way* (1991)?
15 Who proved *Hard to Kill* (1990)?
16 Who had *The Gift* (2000)?
17 Who fled *Into the Night* (1985)?
18 Who was *Down and Out in Beverly Hills* (1986)?
19 Who wanted a *Green Card* (1990)?
20 Who wanted *A Life Less Ordinary* (1997)?
21 Who was *Her Alibi* (1989)?
22 Who was *Castaway* (2000)?
23 Who was *Driving Miss Daisy* (1989)?
24 Who was *Unfaithful* (2002)?
25 Who'd *Never Been Kissed* (1999)?
26 Who wore *The Tuxedo* (2002)?
27 Who was *Guarding Tess* (1994)?
28 Who was *Under Suspicion* (2000)?
29 Who became an *Enemy of the State* (1998)?
30 Who was *Dying Young* (1991)?

❓ 4 SAME OLD, SAME OLD

Same characters, virtually the same story and enough publicity to help ensure the same box office receipts as the original. When Hollywood wants to make a quick buck, but has no idea how to do it ... they make A SEQUEL.

4.1 – SUBTITLES

Sequels often keep the same title as the original; only a number and the occasional subtitle are added to distinguish it from its predecessor. Can you remember the subtitles to these famous (and not so famous) sequels?

1   *Sister Act 2* ... (1993)
2   *City Slickers II* ... (1994)
3   *Superman IV* ... (1987)
4   *Arthur 2* ... (1988)
5   *Terminator 3* ... (2003)
6   *Home Alone 2* ... (1992)
7   *Airplane II* ... (1982)
8   *Gremlins 2* ... (1990)
9   *Highlander II* ... (1991)
10 *Homeward Bound II* ... (1996)
11 *White Fang II* ... (1994)
12 *F/X 2* ... (1991)
13 *Hellraiser III* ... (1992)
14 *Legally Blonde 2* ... (2003)
15 *Spy Kids 2* ... (2002)

4.2 – SOMETHING DIFFERENT

Instead of the all-too-easy way of just adding a number and/or subtitle to the original film title, sometimes – but only sometimes – Hollywood opts for a slightly different title for a sequel. Not sufficiently different to confuse the audience but different enough to show the world there's still a little imagination left in Tinseltown. Can you remember the name of that very similar sounding original film title?

1 *I Still Know What You Did Last Summer* (1998)
2 *2 Fast 2 Furious* (2003)
3 *Honey, I Blew Up the Kid* (1992)
4 *A Very Brady Sequel* (1996)
5 *The Whole Ten Yards* (2003)

The other way around this time. What was the name of the sequel?

6 *The Poseidon Adventure* (1972)
7 *The Guns of Navarone* (1961)
8 *American Graffiti* (1973)
9 *The Bridge on the River Kwai* (1957)
10 *The Wizard of Oz* (1939)

Only very occasionally will Hollywood surprise everyone with a completely different title for a sequel. How surprised were you? What was the name of the original film?

11 *The Two Jakes* (1990)
12 *Texasville* (1990)
13 *Staying Alive* (1983)
14 *The Evening Star* (1996)
15 *Oliver's Story* (1978)

4.3 – THE NUMBERS

Fifteen famous series of films. Just how many of each have been made . . . so far?

1 *Robocop*
2 *Rocky*
3 *Police Academy*
4 *Karate Kid*
5 *Halloween*
6 *Children of the Corn*
7 *My Girl*
8 *Muppet Movies*
   . . . and how many of them can you remember the name of?
9 *Alien*
10 *Poltergeist*
11 *Jaws*
12 *Mad Max*
13 *Iron Eagle*
14 *Rugrats*
15 *Scary Movie*

4.4 – FIRST THINGS FIRST

Which of these similarly titled films was first to reach the big screen?

1 *Bill & Ted's Excellent Adventure* or *Bill & Ted's Bogus Journey*
2 *Every Which Way But Loose* or *Any Which Way You Can*
3 *Analyze That* or *Analyze This*
4 *Escape from New York* or *Escape from L.A.*
5 *Conan the Destroyer* or *Conan the Barbarian*
6 *Three Men and a Little Lady* or *Three Men and a Baby*

7 *Look Who's Talking Too* or *Look Who's Talking Now*
8 *Matrix Reloaded* or *Matrix Revolutions*
9 *An American Werewolf in Paris* or *An American Werewolf in London*
10 *Shanghai Knights* or *Shanghai Noon*

4.5 – THE IMPOSTER

1 Which one of these films was *not* a sequel to the other?

    (a) *Another 48 Hrs.* (1990) to *48 Hrs.* (1982)
    (b) *Next Friday* (2000) to *Friday* (1995)
    (c) *28 Days Later* (2002) to *28 Days* (2000)
    (d) *Grumpier Old Men* (1995) to *Grumpy Old Men* (1993)
    (e) *Gregory's Two Girls* (1999) to *Gregory's Girl* (1981)

2 Despite what you might think, one of these films wasn't someone or something returning for a sequel. Which one?

    (a) The Mummy in *The Mummy Returns* (2001)
    (b) Max Dugan in *Max Dugan Returns* (1983)
    (c) The Black Stallion in *The Black Stallion Returns* (1983)
    (d) The Living Dead in *The Return of the Living Dead* (1985)
    (e) The Swamp Thing in *The Return of the Swamp Thing* (1989)

3 Which of these *A Nightmare On Elm Street* 'adventures' has an incorrect subtitle?

    (a) #2 – Freddy Lives (1985)
    (b) #3 – Dream Warriors (1987)
    (c) #4 – The Dream Master (1988)
    (d) #5 – The Dream Child (1989)
    (e) #6 – Freddy's Dead (1991)

4 Roman numerals. One of these sequels didn't use Roman numerals in its title. Which one?

(a) *Caddyshack II* (1988)
(b) *The Odd Couple II* (1998)
(c) *Weekend at Bernies II* (1993)
(d) *Final Destination II* (2003)
(e) *Crocodile Dundee II* (1988)

5 Which is the sequel in amongst all of these prequels?

(a) *Indiana Jones and the Temple of Doom* (1984)
(b) *Ripley's Game* (2002)
(c) *The Flintstones in Viva Rock Vegas* (2000)
(d) *Dumb & Dumberer* (2003)
(e) *Red Dragon* (2002)

4.6 – THE TRIVIA

1 What was so special about the 1981 Mel Brooks comedy *History of the World Part 1*?
2 Freddy and Jason finally stopped slaughtering high school kids and fought each other instead in which 2003 spin-off?
3 Who was in the wrong place at the wrong time on a bus in 1994 and again three years later on the cruise ship *Seabourn Legend*?
4 What were Orthanc and Minas Morgul better known as?
5 Which famous Italian actor played the part of the legendary Inspector Clouseau's son in the ill-advised sequel, *Son of the Pink Panther* (1993)?
6 Lt. Frank Drebin foiled an assassination attempt on the life of which V.I.P. in *The Naked Gun* (1988)?
7 Where was the Griswald family's first stop on their European vacation?

8 Who was the innocent man on the run from US Marshall Tommy Lee Jones in the 1998 sequel to *The Fugitive*?

9 During his last crusade, Indiana Jones inadvertently collected the autograph of which infamous person?

10 What was the name of the guy in the painting in *Ghostbusters II* (1989)?

11 What was the name of the theme park in *Beverly Hills Cop III* (1994)?

12 Which *Lethal Weapon* film featured the 'bomb-in-the-toilet' gag?

13 What was Isla Sorna better known as?

14 What followed *Koyaanisqatsi* (1983) and *Powaqqatsi* (1988)?

15 What was the title of the third slice of *American Pie*?

And finally . . .

An unbelievably bad and unfunny 2001 Danny DeVito/Martin Lawrence 'comedy' release had as its title a rather embarrassing question: *What's the Worst That Could Happen?* With which obvious two-word answer did some film critics find it hard to resist using to begin their reviews?

❓ 5 FIFTY FIFTY

Decide which of the two possible answers is connected (loosely or otherwise) to the film . . . and why.

1 *40 Days and 40 Nights* (2002): Sex *or* Chocolate
2 *I Am Sam* (2001): Burger King *or* Starbucks
3 *Small Time Crooks* (2000): Sandwiches *or* Cookies
4 *The Shawshank Redemption* (1994): Rita Hayworth *or* Jane Russell
5 *Good Will Hunting* (1997): M.I.T. *or* Harvard
6 *Point Break* (1991): Ex-Wives *or* Ex-Presidents
7 *Sliding Doors* (1998): Elevator *or* Train
8 *Taking Care of Business* (1990): Filofax *or* Laptop
9 *True Romance* (1993): Frank Sinatra *or* Elvis Presley
10 *My Cousin Vinny* (1992): Alabama *or* Arkansas
11 *Three Kings* (1999): Diamonds *or* Gold
12 *The Wedding Planner* (2001): Monopoly *or* Scrabble
13 *Windtalkers* (2002): Navajo *or* Sioux
14 *Star Trek IV – The Voyage Home* (1986): Dolphins *or* Whales
15 *Bustin' Loose* (1981): Bus *or* Train
16 *Minority Report* (2002): Spiders *or* Snakes
17 *Quiz Show* (1994): 21 *or* Jeopardy
18 *The Insider* (2000): Coffee *or* Cigarettes
19 *Alive* (1993): Rugby *or* Hockey
20 *A Private Function* (1984): Pigs *or* Cows
21 *What Women Want* (2002): Reebok *or* Nike
22 *Rounders* (1998): Cards *or* Dice
23 *Rain Man* (1988): Quantas *or* Lufthansa
24 *Bulworth* (1998): Republican *or* Democrat
25 *The Thomas Crown Affair* (1999): Monet *or* Van Gogh
26 *Planes, Trains and Automobiles* (1987): Christmas *or* Thanksgiving
27 *Back to the Future Part III* (1990): John Wayne *or* Clint Eastwood
28 *The Luzhin Defence* (2000): Fencing *or* Chess

29 *Mr Baseball* (1992): Japan *or* Korea
30 *Scent of a Woman* (1992): Tango *or* Waltz

? **6 LINKS**

6.1 – THE COMMON ONE

Find the ONE WORD needed to complete the titles of two different films.

1 needful and very bad
2 ordinary and ruthless
3 on the side and next door
4 with a stranger and with me
5 cowboys and truckers
6 velvet and steel
7 hard and black
8 desperate and extreme
9 in the sky and down below
10 dreams and liberty

6.2 – THE MISSING ONE

Find the MISSING WORD needed to reveal the titles of two different films.

1 something ... at heart
2 forever ... doctors in love
3 blow ... for justice
4 milk ... train
5 fly away ... for the holidays
6 everybody's all ... heart
7 bad ... business
8 the emperor's ... paradise
9 sleepy ... man
10 while you were ... with the enemy

7 TAGLINES

The catchy little phrase that adorns the poster; that little bit extra that's supposed to make you want to see the film.

Think carefully about the taglines listed below to identify a particular film. It's not always that easy, but at least some of them are guessable. The clue is often in the question!

1   Protecting the Earth from the scum of the Universe.
2   Five criminals. One line up. No coincidence.
3   LoveHateDreamsLifeWorkPlayFriendshipSex
4   'As far back as I can remember, I've always wanted to be a gangster . . .'
5   Off the record, on the QT and very hush-hush.
6   Nice planet. We'll take it.
7   A Monk. A Punk. A Chick. In a kick-ass flick.
8   Someone has taken their love of sequels one step too far.
9   If Nancy doesn't wake up screaming . . . she won't wake up at all.
10 Tea at Four. Dinner at Eight. Murder at Midnight.
11 Oceans rise. Cities fall. Hope survives.
12 David is 11 years old. He weighs 60 pounds. He is 4 feet 6 inches tall. He has brown hair. His love is real, but he is not.
13 The fastest hands in the East meet the biggest mouth in the West.
14 Drink from me and live forever.
15 It was supposed to be the safest room in the house.
16 In October 1994, three student filmmakers disappeared in the woods near Burkittesville, Maryland, while shooting a documentary. One year later, their footage was found.
17 Part man. Part machine. All cop. The future of law enforcement.
18 Chucky gets lucky.
19 Hang up and you die.
20 He loved the American dream with a vengeance.
21 Stealing, cheating, killing. Who said romance is dead?

?

22 6 contestants, 6 guns, no rules!
23 If you can't be famous ... be infamous!
24 Man is the warmest place to hide.
25 Do you hate spiders? Do you really hate spiders? Well, they don't like you either!
26 NYC '77. Disco in the clubs. Panic in the streets.
27 Alcatraz. Only one man has ever broken out. Now five million lives depend on two men breaking in.
28 The Hustler isn't what he used to be, but he has the next best thing: a kid who is.
29 She's a fabulous, loving, caring mother, who, er ... happens to be a serial killer!
30 Meet Larry the Liquidator. Arrogant. Greedy. Self-centred. Ruthless. You gotta love the guy.
31 Be afraid ... Be very afraid.
32 Be afraid. Be kind of afraid.
33 ... and hell followed with him.
34 You'll laugh. You'll cry. You'll hurl.
35 On the air. Unaware.
36 Schmidt happens.
37 10 seconds: The pain begins. 15 seconds: You can't breathe. 20 seconds: You explode.
38 Sleep all day, party all night ... It's fun to be a vampire.
39 Silent. Invisible. Invincible. He's in town with a few days to kill.
40 Any call can be murder, any stop can be suicide, any night can be the last. And you thought your job was hell?

8 SMART TALK

How well have you remembered some of those memorable things people have said in the movies? All you have to do is identify the particular film from which these lines of dialogue were taken.

1 I see dead people.
2 I don't understand. All my life I've been waiting for someone and when I find her, she's . . . she's a fish!
3 Snakes. Why'd it have to be snakes?
4 AK-47. When you absolutely, positively got to kill every motherfucker in the room. Accept no substitutes.
5 Stanley, see this? This is this! This ain't something else, this is this!
6 I was in the Virgin Islands once. I met a girl. We ate lobster and drank pina coladas. At sunset we made love like sea otters. Why couldn't I get that day over and over . . . ?
7 You're not very bright, are you? I like that in a man.
8 Lads do football or boxing or wrestling . . . not ballet.
9 He's not the Messiah, he's a very naughty boy!
10 You never got me down, Ray. You never had me down.
11 Nothing like a good piece of hickory!
12 We'd better get back 'cause it'll be dark soon, and they mostly come at night . . . mostly.
13 What came first, the music or the misery? Did I listen to pop music because I was miserable? Or was I miserable because I listened to pop music?
14 Cancel the kitchen scraps for lepers and orphans, no more merciful beheadings . . . and call off Christmas!
15 To infinity and beyond . . .
16 Cocaine. Have you ever fucked on cocaine, Nick? It's nice.
17 When people ask me if Michael Sullivan was a good man, or if there was no good in him at all, I always give the same answer. I just tell them: he was my father.

18 I came here tonight because when you realise you want to spend the rest of your life with somebody, you want the rest of your life to start as soon as possible.

19 I can't listen to that much Wagner, ya know? I start to get the urge to conquer Poland.

20 This is a full-blown, four-alarm holiday emergency here! We're gonna press on, and we're gonna have the hap ... hap ... happiest Christmas since Bing Crosby tap-danced with Danny fucking Kaye!

21 Mr Brown? That sounds too much like Mr Shit.

22 I'm the ghost with the most, babe!

23 You wanna see something really scary?

24 That's more than a dress. That's an Audrey Hepburn movie!

25 Every minute I stay in this room, I get weaker, and every minute Charlie squats in the bush, he gets stronger.

26 Frank, if somebody requested 'Chopsticks' you'd ask for the sheet music.

27 We came, we saw, we kicked its ass!

28 Women need a reason for having sex; men just need a place.

29 Can I get ya anything? Coffee? Tea? Me?

30 You want to explain the math of this to me? I mean, where's the sense in risking the lives of the eight of us to save one guy?

31 You mean, y'all paid, what, $80,000 for this car and you ain't got no damn cup holder?

32 I'd be the worst possible Godfather. I'd forget all her birthdays until she was 18. Then I'd take her out and get her drunk ... and, let's face it, quite probably try and shag her.

33 I have an interesting case. I'm treating two sets of Siamese twins with split personalities. I'm getting paid by eight people.

34 The point is, ladies and gentlemen, that greed, for lack of a better word, is good. Greed is right. Greed works.

35 That's all you got, lady. Two wrong feet, in fucking ugly shoes!

36 I own the hotel and live there. So you can pretty much say that my life is like Monopoly.

37 This is a real badge, I'm a real cop, and this is a real fuckin' gun!

38 The Germans and the Italians couldn't get rid of us. There is absolutely no reason why we should surrender to the Scots.

39 I want this guy dead. I want his family dead. I want his house burned to the ground. I want to go there in the middle of the night and piss on his ashes!

40 I always thought it would be better to be a fake somebody than a real nobody.

41 You know something, you ain't nothing special. You got no manners, you treat women like whores and if you ask me you got no chance of being no officer.

42 I came home to raise crops, and God willing, a family. If I can live in peace, I will.

43 No matter what anybody tells you, words and ideas can change the world.

44 I'm just a little anxious to get up there and whup ET's ass!

45 Free cable is the ultimate aphrodisiac.

?•? 9 THE CASTING COUCH

9.1 – TO DIE FOR

Identify the film from its cast of leading actors.

1 Billy Crystal, John Cusack, Julia Roberts, Catherine Zeta-Jones, Christopher Walken, Alan Arkin.
2 Michelle Pfeiffer, Glenn Close, John Malkovich, Swoosie Kurtz, Keanu Reeves, Uma Thurman.
3 Robert Duvall, Richard Harris, Shirley MacLaine, Sandra Bullock.
4 Kiefer Sutherland, Julia Roberts, Kevin Bacon, William Baldwin, Oliver Platt.
5 Gene Hackman, Angelica Huston, Gwyneth Paltrow, Ben Stiller, Bill Murray, Danny Glover, Owen Wilson.
6 Jeff Bridges, John Goodman, Julianne Moore, John Turturro, Steve Buscemi, Philip Seymour Hoffman.
7 Bruce Willis, Billy Bob Thornton, Cate Blanchett.
8 Kevin Costner, Kevin Bacon, Tommy Lee Jones, Gary Oldman, Joe Pesci, John Candy, Jack Lemmon, Walter Matthau, Donald Sutherland, Sissy Spacek, Vincent D'Onofrio, Lolita Davidovich.
9 Robert De Niro, Edward Norton, Marlon Brando, Angela Bassett.
10 Dustin Hoffman, Rene Russo, Morgan Freeman, Kevin Spacey, Cuba Gooding Jr, Donald Sutherland.
11 Danny Glover, Kevin Kline, Steve Martin, Mary McDonnell, Mary Louise Parker, Alfre Woodard.
12 Sean Penn, Nick Nolte, Jennifer Lopez, Powers Boothe, Claire Danes, Joaquin Phoenix, Billy Bob Thornton.
13 Jon Voight, Eric Roberts, Rebecca De Mornay.
14 Jane Fonda, Alan Alda, Maggie Smith, Michael Caine, Walter Matthau, Richard Pryor, Bill Cosby.
15 Sally Field, Dolly Parton, Shirley MacLaine, Daryl Hannah, Olympia Dukakis, Julia Roberts, Tom Skerritt, Sam Shepard, Dylan McDermott, Kevin J. O'Connor.

16 Bridget Fonda, Matt Dillon, Campbell Scott, Kyra Sedgwick, Bill Pullman, Eric Stoltz.

17 Liv Tyler, Jeremy Irons, Joseph Fiennes, Sinéad Cusack, Rachel Weisz.

18 Robert Redford, Robert Duvall, Glenn Close, Kim Basinger, Wilford Brimley, Barbara Hershey, Richard Farnsworth.

19 Jack Nicholson, Kathleen Turner, Angelica Huston.

20 Jude Law, Nicole Kidman, Renée Zellweger, Natalie Portman, Philip Seymour Hoffman, Donald Sutherland.

21 Leonardo Di Caprio, Jeremy Irons, John Malkovich, Gérard Depardieu, Gabriel Byrne, Anne Parillaud.

22 Sam Neill, Nicole Kidman, Billy Zane.

23 Jennifer Lopez, Ralph Fiennes, Natasha Richardson, Bob Hoskins, Stanley Tucci.

24 Madeleine Stowe, Mary Stuart Masterson, Andie MacDowell, Drew Barrymore, Robert Loggia, Dermot Mulroney.

25 Sean Penn, Adrien Brody, James Caviezel, Ben Chaplin, George Clooney, John Cusack, Woody Harrelson, Nick Nolte, John Travolta, John C. Reilly, John Savage.

9.2 – ONE TIME ONLY

These Hollywood 'heavyweights' have been seen together only once on screen. What was the title of that movie?

1 Clint Eastwood and Kevin Costner
2 Dustin Hoffman and Gene Hackman
3 Al Pacino and Robert De Niro
4 Sean Connery and Michelle Pfeiffer
5 Julia Roberts and Mel Gibson
6 Tom Cruise and Jack Nicholson
7 Bruce Willis and Richard Gere

8 Tom Hanks and Denzel Washington
9 Harrison Ford and Brad Pitt
10 Marlon Brando and George C. Scott

9.3 – DEJA VU

Some people, on the other hand, just can't get enough of each other. They don't just work together the once, but again ... and sometimes, again and again. From the following list of movies, identify the two stars who keep meeting up on the big screen.

1 *Stakeout* (1987), *Blink* (1994)
2 *School Ties* (1992), *Chasing Amy* (1997), *Good Will Hunting* (1997), *Dogma* (1999), *Jersey Girl* (2004)
3 *Silver Streak* (1976), *Stir Crazy* (1980), *See No Evil, Hear No Evil* (1989), *Another You* (1991)
4 *Frances* (1982), *Country* (1984), *Crimes of the Heart* (1986)
5 *Cannery Row* (1982), *Everybody Wins* (1990)
6 *No Mercy* (1986), *Final Analysis* (1992)
7 *Howards End* (1992), *The Remains of the Day* (1993)
8 *Innerspace* (1987), *D.O.A* (1988), *Flesh and Bone* (1993)
9 *The Deer Hunter* (1978), *Falling in Love* (1984), *Marvin's Room* (1996)
10 *Little Shop of Horrors* (1986), *Parenthood* (1989), *My Blue Heaven* (1990), *L.A. Story* (1991)

9.4 – AGAINST TYPE

Some people are always associated with a certain type of role: Chevy Chase always plays the part of a wise-ass, Hugh Grant is a floppy-haired dandy and Arnie never stops killing bad guys. Sometimes, they can't resist trying to change a winning formula and start doing all manner of strange things for the sake of wanting to be different. Jean-Claude Van Damme hasn't done comedy yet, but can it be long before he does? The world holds its breath.

Can you remember the name of the film in which the following actors became famous for not playing the type of role for which they originally became famous?

1 Steve Martin – being serious
2 Denzel Washington – as a corrupt cop
3 Robin Williams – as a seriously deranged shop assistant
4 Keanu Reeves – as a serial killer
5 Michael J. Fox – as a G.I. in a gritty Vietnam war drama
6 Roger Moore – as a Nazi officer
7 Pierce Brosnan – as an American Indian fur trapper
8 Laurence Olivier – in a film adaptation of a Harold Robbins novel
9 Goldie Hawn – in a thriller (and not playing the role of a dizzy blonde)
10 Fred Astaire – in a spooky little horror film

9.5 – SMALL BEGINNINGS

Which of today's big names had these less than impressive starts to their careers? Without a clue it would be impossible, with a clue, it's still not easy!

1 Courtroom observer in *The Verdict* (1982)
    Before he became TV's David Addison.
2 Pretty girl on train in *Stardust Memories* (1980)
    She later uncrossed her legs . . . and the rest is movie history!
3 Man in alley in *Frances* (1982)
    The dead guy from *The Big Chill* (1983).
4 Boy getting haircut in *Coming to America* (1988)
    Show him the money!
5 Woman in elevator in *Deconstructing Harry* (1997)
    No relation to James.

10   10 × 10

?°?

10.1 – MR PRESIDENT

Which actors have played the role of the President of the United States (real or imaginary) in the following films?

1 *Air Force One* (1997)
2 *The American President* (1995)
3 *Deep Impact* (1998)
4 *Mars Attacks!* (1996)
5 *Dave* (1993)
6 *Independence Day* (1996)
7 *Nixon* (1995)
8 *Pearl Harbor* (2001)
9 *Executive Target* (1997)
10 *Absolute Power* (1997)

10.2 – DON'T THEY MAKE A LOVELY COUPLE

Who played these famous screen couples and in which films did they appear?

1 Alabama Whitman and Clarence Worley
2 Cora Papadakis and Frank Chambers
3 Karen Sisco and Jack Foley
4 Honey Bunny and Pumpkin
5 Mallory and Mickey Knox
6 Ethel and Norman Thayer
7 Dixie Leonard and Eddie Sparks
8 Lula Fortune and Sailor Ripley
9 Molly Jensen and Sam Wheat
10 Baby Houseman and Johnny Castle

10.3 – VILLAINS

Who played the 'bad guy' in these films?

1 *The Fifth Element* (1997)
2 *Lock Up* (1989)
3 *In the Line of Fire* (1993)
4 *Arlington Road* (1999)
5 *The Hand that Rocks the Cradle* (1992)
6 *Cliffhanger* (1993)
7 *Breakdown* (1997)
8 *Unlawful Entry* (1992)
9 *Pacific Heights* (1990)
10 *Kiss of Death* (1995)

10.4 – TOUGH GUYS

Arnie, Sly and Jean-Claude have kicked a lot of ass in their time. Which one of them was doing the kicking in these films?

1 *Collateral Damage* (2002)
2 *Cobra* (1986)
3 *Eraser* (1996)
4 *Sudden Death* (1995)
5 *End of Days* (1999)
6 *Timecop* (1994)
7 *Death Warrant* (1990)
8 *D-Tox* (2002)
9 *Assassins* (1995)
10 *Commando* (1985)

10.5 – NOM DE PLUME

What were these characters better known as?

1 Jay and Kay
2 Kris Kringle
3 Alexandra Medford, Jane Spofford and Sukie Ridgemont
4 Dusty Bottoms, Lucky Day and Ned Nederlander
5 Kal-El and Kara Zor-El
6 Mick Shrimpton, Viv Savage, Nigel Tufnel, David St Hubbins and Derek Smalls
7 Blossom, Bubbles and Buttercup
8 Experiment #626
9 Don Diego de la Vega
10 Eliot Ness, Jim Malone, George Stone and Oscar Wallace

10.6 – FRIEND OR FOE

These guys were either best buddies or spent the whole movie bickering and fighting with each other. Identify if they were FRIEND or FOE, who played the roles and in which film?

1 Bill 'BB' Babowsky and Ernest Tilley
2 Gavin Banek and Doyle Gipson
3 Col. Knowles and Col. Valachev
4 Felix Unger and Oscar Madison
5 Amsterdam Vallon and William Cutting
6 Romy White and Michelle Weinberger
7 Lawrence Jamieson and Freddy Benson
8 Jack Walsh and Jonathan Mardukas
9 Barbara and Oliver Rose
10 'Harley Davidson' and 'The Marlboro Man'

10.7 – CREDIT WHERE CREDIT'S DUE

It may be them doing a favour for a director friend or just being at a loose end for a couple of days between movies. Whatever the reason, Hollywood types all like to do the odd uncredited cameo every so often. Which big name star has appeared in the following films in an uncredited role?

1 *Robin Hood – Prince of Thieves* (1991)
   Clue: Richard the Lionheart
2 *Notting Hill* (1999)
   Clue: Jeff King, Anna Scott's obnoxious boyfriend
3 *A Night at the Roxbury* (1998)
   Clue: Mr Zadir, the owner of The Roxbury
4 *Maverick* (1994)
   Clue: A bank robber
5 *The Adventures of Rocky and Bullwinkle* (2000)
   Clue: A mattress salesman
6 *Bordello of Blood* (1996)
   Clue: A hospital patient
7 *Cold Feet* (1989)
   Clue: A bartender
8 *National Lampoon's Loaded Weapon 1* (1993)
   Clue: A man with a car phone
9 *Young Guns* (1988)
   Clue: A cowboy
10 *Fathers' Day* (1997)
   Clue: Scott, the body piercer

10.8 – NICKNAMES

Who played these famous 'nicknamed' characters and in which films?

1 Mae 'All-The-Way-Mae' Mordabito
2 Cyrus 'The Virus' Grissom
3 Archibald 'Moonlight' Graham
4 Rick 'Wild Thing' Vaughn
5 'Quiz Kid' Donnie Smith
6 Wade 'Cry-Baby' Walker
7 Randall 'Memphis' Raines
8 Sam 'Ace' Rothstein
9 'Shopgirl' and 'NY152'
10 'D-Fens'

10.9 – THE SUPPORT

It's not always the star names above the title that grab all the headlines. Sometimes, those actors with a supporting role can be just as memorable. Who played these famous supporting characters and in which films?

1 Leo Getz
2 Felicity Shagwell
3 George Downes
4 Garrett Breedlove
5 Tina Carlyle
6 Oda Mae Brown
7 Jesus Quintana
8 Early Grace
9 English Bob
10 Sharon Stone

10.10 – FAMOUS NAMES

Who played these famous people?

1 Charlie Chaplin in *Chaplin* (1992)
2 Tina Turner in *What's Love Got to Do with It* (1993)
3 Muhammad Ali in *Ali* (2001)
4 Joan Crawford in *Mommie Dearest* (1981)
5 Charlie Parker in *Bird* (1988)
6 Jerry Lee Lewis in *Great Balls of Fire!* (1989)
7 D.H. Lawrence in *Priest of Love* (1981)
8 Ludwig Van Beethoven in *Immortal Beloved* (1994)
9 Joan Of Arc in *The Messenger* (1999)
10 Geronimo in *Geronimo – An American Legend* (1993)

11   BODY PARTS

Find the missing word(s) to complete the film title. How simple is that?

1   *Fort Apache ... (1981)*
2   *Life or Something ... (2003)*
3   *Chicago Joe and ... (1990)*
4   *Eternal Sunshine ... (2003)*
5   *Along Came ... (2001)*
6   *All the Pretty ... (2000)*
7   *And Justice ... (1979)*
8   *My Big Fat ... (2002)*
9   *South Park: ... (1999)*
10 *Things You Can Only Tell ... (2000)*
11 *Jo Jo Dancer, ... (1986)*
12 *What Dreams ... (1998)*
13 *At Play in the Fields ... (1991)*
14 *Bodies, Rest and ... (1993)*
15 *Gas Food ... (1992)*
16 *Midnight in the Garden ... (1997)*
17 *To Wong Foo, Thanks for Everything, ... (1995)*
18 *Merry Christmas, ... (1982)*
19 *Divine Secrets of ... (2002)*
20 *Even Cowgirls ... (1993)*
21 *Where the Day ... (1992)*
22 *My Own Private ... (1991)*
23 *Come Back to the 5 and Dime ... (1982)*
24 *Sweet Home ... (2002)*
25 *In Praise of ... (1978)*
26 *Five Days ... (1982)*
27 *So I Married ... (1993)*
28 *How Stella ... (1998)*
29 *Snow Falling ... (1999)*

30 *Last Exit to . . .* (1989)
31 *When the Whales . . .* (1989)
32 *Things to Do in Denver . . .* (1995)
33 *Don't Tell Mom . . .* (1991)
34 *Children of a Lesser . . .* (1986)
35 *Something Wicked . . .* (1983)
36 *Full Moon in . . .* (1988)
37 *To Live and Die . . .* (1985)
38 *Stop! . . .* (1992)
39 *Fear and Loathing . . .* (1998)
40 *Twin Peaks: . . .* (1992)

12　WHAT WAS WHAT

1　What was *Memphis Belle* (1990)?
2　What was *The Mexican* (2001)?
3　What was *Event Horizon* (1997)?
4　What was *Blue Thunder* (1983)?
5　What was *Christine* (1983)?
6　What was *K-Pax* (2001)?
7　What were *Fat Man and Little Boy* (1989)?
8　What was *Simpatico* (1999)?
9　What was *The Money Pit* (1986)?
10　What was *Porky's* (1981)?
11　What was *Jumanji* (1995)?
12　What was *Galaxy Quest* (1999)?
13　What was *Brokedown Palace* (1999)?
14　What was *Tron* (1982)?
15　What was *Coyote Ugly* (2000)?
16　What was *Dante's Peak* (1997)?
17　What was *The Skulls* (2000)?
18　What was *The Purple Rose of Cairo* (1985)?
19　What was *Amistad* (1997)?
20　What was *Gattaca* (1997)?
21　What was *Rushmore* (1999)?
22　What was *White Palace* (1990)?
23　What were *The Ghost and the Darkness* (1996)?
24　What was *Deathtrap* (1982)?
25　What was *The Big Red One* (1980)?
26　What was *The Package* (1989)?
27　What was *Fatal Beauty* (1987)?
28　What was *Sharky's Machine* (1981)?
29　What was *That Thing You Do!* (1996)?
30　What was *Widows' Peak* (1994)?

And finally . . .

What was *The Matrix* (1999–2003)?

❓ 13 SHORT AND SWEET

Everything that's not always that simple!

1. What becomes her?
2. Do what?
3. Bondi, Waikiki and Venice, to name but a few
4. Something very simple
5. 3.14159 . . .
6. Who got the blame?
7. Every February 2nd
8. 'Once upon a time, there were 3 little girls . . .'
9. XES
10. For the love of what?
11. What you might pay extra for in a hotel
12. Paris. It ain't in France. So where is it?
13. Who ya gonna call . . . and what's their number?
14. Where did Betty Lou hide the gun?
15. Ready To Wear
16. Tough Guys don't do it
17. How old was Gillian?
18. False truths, it ain't
19. Exit Blocked
20. . . . the night before.
21. Time spent by the lake in the country
22. Every parents' nightmare (especially on Christmas morning)
23. White men can't do it
24. ZOO
25. What happened to Peggy Sue?
26. His favourite year?
27. ANG L
28. Office hours
29. . . . and fancy free.

30 Bert Rigby. A genius or a fool?
31 ... And what about that kid, Jimmy Neutron?
32 Mickey's eyes and the Devil's dress
33 A hobby for geeks
34 Sleepless nights
35 A party that Mike and Sully might attend
36 A cheerful little town in Texas
37 A famous red windmill
38 It's not sticky, but you can get stuck in it
39 7.12.41
40 Who stole Christmas?
41 ... and who saved it?
42 English and Handsome
43 Yellow, Blue and Red
44 Trepidation + Apprehension + Fright + Terror =
45 Somewhere midway between Red and Blue
46 The 24 equal parts of a day
47 ... + Spike's extra one
48 A famous Leonardo da Vinci painting
49 Stuck for words
50 WHAT

1 *HARRY POTTER* (2001–05)
Which of these names was not one of the four houses at Hogwarts school?

(a) Gryffindor
(b) Slytherin
(c) Phindroll
(d) Ravenclaw
(e) Hufflepuff

2 OLD TV SHOWS
Which classic old TV show hasn't yet been adapted for the big screen?

(a) *X Files* (1993–2002)
(b) *Dragnet* (1951–59)
(c) *Sgt Bilko* (1955–59)
(d) *Hogan's Heroes* (1965–71)
(e) *Maverick* (1957–62)

3 *OCEAN'S ELEVEN* (2001)
Which Las Vegas casino wasn't on Danny Ocean's list of targets to rob?

(a) Bellagio
(b) Luxor
(c) MGM Grand
(d) Mirage

4 *ROCKY* (1976–90)
Which of these characters hasn't been an opponent for 'Rocky' Balboa?

(a) Cesar Dominguez

(b) Ivan Drago
(c) Clubber Lang
(d) Apollo Creed

5 *X-MEN* (2000–03)
Who was not an X-Man ... or woman?

(a) Storm
(b) Wolverine
(c) Rogue
(d) Cyclops
(e) Mystique

6 POOR COW
In which film did the poor unfortunate cow actually escape a sudden and untimely death?

(a) By drowning in *O Brother, Where Art Thou?* (2000)
(b) Being caught in a hurricane in *Twister* (1996)
(c) Being shot in the head (several times) in *Me, Myself & Irene* (2000)
(d) By stepping on a landmine in *Three Kings* (1999)

7 VIDEO GAMES
Which of these films was not inspired by a video game?

(a) *Super Mario Bros.* (1993)
(b) *Mortal Kombat* (1995)
(c) *Resident Evil* (2002)
(d) *The Scorpion King* (2002)
(e) *Street Fighter* (1994)

8 *AIRPLANE* (1980)
Which of these nasty little habits didn't Steve McCrosky pick the wrong day to quit?

(a) Glue sniffing
(b) Swearing
(c) Drinking
(d) Amphetamines
(e) Smoking

9 *RESERVOIR DOGS* (1992)
Which colour wasn't used as an alias?

(a) Pink
(b) Blonde
(c) Black
(d) Orange
(e) White

10 *FIGHT CLUB* (1999)
Which of these wasn't a rule of Fight Club?

(a) You do not talk about Fight Club.
(b) When someone says stop, goes limp or taps out, the fight is over.
(c) Fights go on as long as they have to.
(d) No video, no photos, no publicity.
(e) If it's your fight night at Fight Club, you have to fight.

11 *LIFE OF BRIAN* (1979)
What didn't the Romans give them?

(a) Irrigation
(b) Sanitation

(c) Medicine
(d) Health Insurance
(e) Public order

12 *THE FAMILY MAN* (2000)
What wasn't suddenly a part of Jack Campbell's new life?

(a) A broken down mini-van
(b) A job at Ed's Tyre Mart
(c) A house in suburbia
(d) A mother-in-law 'from hell'
(e) A wife and two kids

13 VILLAINOUS FELINES
In which film was the cat actually a good guy?

(a) Smokey in *Stuart Little* (1999)
(b) Mr Tinkles in *Cats & Dogs* (2001)
(c) Sassy in *Homeward Bound* (1993–96)
(d) Duchess in *Babe* (1995)
(e) Cat R. Waul in *An American Tail – Fievel Goes West* (1991)

14 SHARON STONE
In which film didn't we see a bit or all of the lovely Ms Stone?

(a) *The Specialist* (1994)
(b) *Diabolique* (1996)
(c) *Sliver* (1993)
(d) *Intersection* (1994)
(e) *Basic Instinct* (1992)

15 DON'T LOSE YOUR HEAD
Who didn't literally lose their head?

(a) Christian Slater in *Windtalkers* (2002)
(b) Andy Garcia in *Black Rain* (1989)
(c) Dennis Hopper in *Speed* (1994)
(d) Denzel Washington in *Fallen* (1998)
(e) Ian Holm in *Alien* (1979)

16 *THE SIXTH SENSE* (1999)
Which of these wasn't a clue as to the unfortunate doctor's demise?

(a) He didn't speak to anyone else but the kid.
(b) Anti-depressants in the bathroom cabinet.
  – to help the grieving widow cope with her husband's sudden
    and violent death, perhaps?
(c) He couldn't open the door to the basement.
(d) The bus didn't stop to pick him up.
(e) The table was always set for one – at home and in the restaurant.

17 HARVEY KEITEL
In which film didn't Mr Keitel play a cop?

(a) *Rising Sun* (1993)
(b) *Bad Lieutenant* (1992)
(c) *Clockers* (1995)
(d) *Head Above Water* (1996)
(e) *Mortal Thoughts* (1991)

18 *SCOOBY-DOO* (2002–04)
Who wasn't a member of the Mystery Inc. gang?

(a) Shaggy

(b) Daphne

(c) Joey

(d) Fred

(e) Velma

19 *GREMLINS* (1984–90)

Which of these four basic rules wasn't a safeguard against the little critters turning nasty?

(a) No water (i.e. don't get them wet)

(b) No food after midnight

(c) No bright lights

(d) No contact with household pets

20 *TOY STORY* (1995–99)

Who wasn't a regular supporting toy?

(a) Slinky Dog

(b) Sailor Sam

(c) Mr Potato Head

(d) Hamm, the Piggy Bank

(e) Bo Peep

21 MAGIC NUMBER

Stephen King seems to like the number 237. However, which of these examples of its use was not true?

(a) Room #237 – The haunted room at the Overlook Hotel in *The Shining* (1980)

(b) $2.37 – The amount of money collected together by the boys in *Stand by Me* (1986)

(c) Cell #237 – Red's cell number in *The Shawshank Redemption* (1994)

(d) 237 Maple St – Bobby Garfield's address as a kid in *Hearts in Atlantis* (2001)

22 COEN BROTHERS TRICKERY
Which of these in-jokes is untrue?

(a) 'Big Dave' Brewster (James Gandolfini) is seen reading a paperback entitled *Blood Simple* in *The Man Who Wasn't There* (2001)
   – Reference to *Blood Simple* (1984)
(b) H.I. McDonnough (Nicolas Cage) wears a 'Hudsucker Industries' uniform in *Raising Arizona* (1987)
   – Reference to *The Hudsucker Proxy* (1994)
(c) Bernie Bernbaum (John Turturro) arranges to meet somebody at the 'Barton Arms' in *Miller's Crossing* (1990)
   – Reference to *Barton Fink* (1991)

23 WHEN IS A TURTLE NOT A TURTLE?
Which of these guys was not one of the *Teenage Mutant Ninja Turtles* (1990–93)?

(a) Caravaggio
(b) Michelangelo
(c) Donatello
(d) Raphael
(e) Leonardo

24 *TOP GUN* (1986)
Which one of these Top Gun call-signs is the fake?

(a) Maverick – Lt. Pete 'Maverick' Mitchell
(b) Slider - Lt. Ron 'Slider' Kerner
(c) Goose – Lt. Nick 'Goose' Bradshaw

(d) Viper – Comdr. Mike 'Viper' Metcalf
    (e) Tiger – Lt. Comdr. Rick 'Tiger' Heatherly

25 RAZZIES
While The Oscars celebrate the best in film, the Golden Raspberry Awards 'celebrate' the worst. Which one of these films didn't have the dubious honour of picking up a Razzie for Worst Film . . . but probably should have?

    (a) *Can't Stop the Music* (1980)
    (b) *The Lonely Lady* (1983)
    (c) *Bolero* (1984)
    (d) *Barb Wire* (1996)
    (e) *Battlefield Earth* (2000)

26 DATES
Which of these dates wasn't the title of a film?

    (a) *1941* (1979)
    (b) *1969* (1988)
    (c) *2000* (1999)
    (d) *1984* (1984)
    (e) *2010* (1984)

27 A HAIRY BRUCE WILLIS
In which film did Bruce Willis actually appear with a full head of hair?

    (a) *12 Monkeys* (1995)
    (b) *Unbreakable* (2000)
    (c) *Pulp Fiction* (1994)
    (d) *Tears of the Sun* (2003)
    (e) *The Siege* (1998)

28 JOURNALIST TYPES
Who hasn't played the part of a newspaper reporter?

(a) Julia Roberts in *I Love Trouble* (1994)
(b) Sally Field in *Absence of Malice* (1981)
(c) Clint Eastwood in *True Crime* (1999)
(d) Bruce Willis in *The Bonfire of the Vanities* (1990)
(e) James Woods in *Against All Odds* (1984)

29 OLD NICK
Who wasn't a little devil?

(a) Elizabeth Hurley in *Bedazzled* (2000)
(b) Robert De Niro in *Angel Heart* (1987)
(c) Adam Sandler in *Little Nicky* (2000)
(d) Jennifer Love Hewitt in *The Devil and Daniel Webster* (2001)
(e) Al Pacino in *The Devil's Advocate* (1997)

30 CAB RIDE
Night On Earth (1991) told the story of five different cab rides in five different cities around the world. So, which city wasn't one of them?

(a) Los Angeles
(b) New York
(c) Rome
(d) Paris
(e) Helsinki
(f) London

15 GUYS AND DOLLS

15.1 – THE GUYS

Identify the leading man from a list of some of his big-screen lady friends.

1 Debra Winger, Lena Olin, Mary McDonnell and Jane Fonda.
2 Milla Jovovich, Mary Stuart Masterson, Winona Ryder and Samantha Mathis.
3 Sigourney Weaver, Dianne Wiest, Farrah Fawcett and Daryl Hannah.
4 Geneviève Bujold, Jill Clayburgh, Melanie Griffith and Glenn Close.
5 Michelle Pfeiffer, Barbara Hershey, Jane March and Kim Basinger.
6 Mary Steenburgen, Ellen Barkin, Helen Hunt and Diane Keaton.
7 Sean Young, Nicole Kidman, Diane Lane and Kelly Lynch.

15.2 – THE DOLLS

The same thing, but the other way around this time. Identify the leading lady from a compilation of some of her men friends.

1 James Spader, Richard Dreyfuss, William Hurt and Harvey Keitel.
2 Hugh Grant, Ben Affleck, Harry Connick Jr and Bill Pullman.
3 Willem Dafoe, Ed Harris, Patrick Swayze, and Al Pacino.
4 Matthew Broderick, Val Kilmer, Kevin Kline and Kiefer Sutherland.
5 John Malkovich, Liam Neeson, Michael Keaton and Andy Garcia.
6 Gary Oldman, Michael Douglas, Jeff Daniels and Tom Cruise.
7 Charlie Sheen, Dudley Moore, Ben Kingsley and John Savage.

?
16 SIXES AND SEVENS

Identify which film connects each actor to the next in line – as well as the last one back to the first one. It's not as easy as it sounds, that's why a free answer has been included with every question. How generous is that?

Note: The connection can only be made from those films in which the two actors shared starring and/or supporting roles and therefore it doesn't include any cameo performances, voice-overs or appearances in which they are credited as 'themselves'.

1 Harrison Ford
   Gene Wilder
   Charles Grodin
   Martin Short ——————— *Clifford* **(1994)**
   Danny Glover
   Willem Dafoe

2 Alec Baldwin
   Meg Ryan
   Kevin Spacey
   Andy Garcia ——————— *A Show of Force* **(1990)**
   Kenneth Branagh
   Denzel Washington
   Kelly Lynch

3 Whoopi Goldberg
   Elizabeth Perkins
   Alan Arkin ——————— *Indian Summer* **(1993)**
   Marisa Tomei
   Woody Harrelson
   Kiefer Sutherland
   Sally Field

4 John Travolta
Halle Berry
Kurt Russell
Mel Gibson
Jamie Lee Curtis
Linda Fiorentino ———— *Queen's Logic* (1991)

5 Antonio Banderas
Emma Thompson
Jonathan Pryce ———— *Carrington* (1995)
Madonna
Harvey Keitel
Theresa Russell
Jeremy Irons

6 Kevin Kline
Rod Steiger
Charles Bronson ———— *Love and Bullets* (1979)
Lee Marvin
William Hurt
Sigourney Weaver

7 John Cusack
Anjelica Huston
Lena Olin
Claire Danes ———— *Polish Wedding* (1998)
Matt Damon
Charlize Theron
Al Pacino

8 Ed Harris
Madeleine Stowe
Kevin Costner
Elijah Wood
Paul Hogan
Cuba Gooding Jr _____ *Lightning Jack* (1994)
Anthony Hopkins

9 Albert Finney
Tom Courtenay
Bob Hoskins _____ *Last Orders* (2001)
Denzel Washington
Angelina Jolie
David Duchovny
Julia Roberts

10 **Mel Gibson**
Goldie Hawn
Geoffrey Rush
Kate Winslet
Dougray Scott
Tim Roth _____ *The Million Dollar Hotel* (2000)

17 REMAKES

When someone thinks they can do better than the first guy!

17.1 – THE ORIGINALS

Who played their role in the original film?

1 Pierce Brosnan in *The Thomas Crown Affair* (1999)
2 Steve Martin in *Father of the Bride* (1991)
3 Samuel L. Jackson in *Shaft* (2000)
4 Mark Wahlberg in *Planet of the Apes* (2001)
5 Eddie Murphy in *Dr Dolittle* (1998)
6 Winona Ryder in *Little Women* (1994)
7 Jeremy Irons in *Lolita* (1997)
8 Julia Ormond in *Sabrina* (1995)
9 Sharon Stone in *Gloria* (1999)
10 Mel Brooks in *To Be or Not to Be* (1983)
11 Nick Nolte in *Cape Fear* (1991)
12 Denzel Washington in *The Preacher's Wife* (1996)
13 Kim Basinger in *The Getaway* (1994)
14 Warren Beatty in *Heaven Can Wait* (1978)
15 Keanu Reeves in *Sweet November* (2001)

17.2 – NEARLY NEW

Hollywood doesn't always stop at remaking its own. It often trawls through the archives of the European cinema for a suitable film to remake. Nobody would have seen the original since the American audiences are notorious for being scared off by subtitles and unfamiliar 'foreign faces'. What is little more than a rehash of the usually much better original is then marketed as a wonderfully new and exciting all-American blockbuster.

So, how were these subtitled originals retitled for their glossy Hollywood make-overs?

1 *Le Retour De Martin Guerre/The Return Of Martin Guerre* (1982)
2 *Der Himmel Uber Berlin/Wings Of Desire* (1987)
3 *A Bout De Souffle* (1960)
4 *Mon Père, Ce Héros* (1991)
   Who played the same role of 'Mon Père' in both the original and the remake?
5 *Nikita* (1990)

17.3 – THE TRIVIA

1   John McTiernan's 2002 remake of *Rollerball* was relocated, for whatever reason, to which country?

2   The 1988 comedy *Switching Channels* was merely a reworking of the 1931 and 1974 films *The Front Page*. How did the writers change the story to make things a little more up-to-date?

3   Which of these animated films hasn't Walt Disney chosen to remake as a live action feature . . . yet?
    (a)   *The Jungle Book* (1967)
    (b)   *101 Dalmatians* (1961)
    (c)   *The Aristocats* (1970)

4   Which classic Alfred Hitchcock movie did Gus Van Sant remake in 1998? What made it so different from any other remake?

5   Which Italian city was the setting for the original 1969 *Italian Job* and which US city formed the backdrop for the 2003 remake?

6   Which classic Raymond Chandler novel was remade into a film in 1978 with Robert Mitchum playing the part of Philip Marlowe? Why was it just a little different from all the other versions of the story?

7   There are some films they should never remake but they do. Which one of these five classic films received the unwarranted attention of some clueless Hollywood producer, which then resulted in a totally unnecessary and inept remake that nobody went to see?
    (a)   *Get Carter* (1971)
    (b)   *The Dirty Dozen* (1967)
    (c)   *From Here To Eternity* (1953)
    (d)   *Willy Wonka & the Chocolate Factory* (1971)
    (e)   *The Sound Of Music* (1965)

8   What was the name of the *Village of the Damned* (1960/1995) where all the young women suddenly gave birth to creepy little blonde babies?

9 What was the name of the old lady who vanished from the train in 1938 and again in 1979?

10 How many versions of the John Buchan novel *The Thirty-Nine Steps* have made it to the big screen and which actors have played the role of Richard Hannay?

11 *Love Affair* (1994) was a rather unsuccessful remake of which 1950s weepie? In which 1993 chick flick did Meg Ryan and Rosie O'Donnell become a little emotional while watching the original on TV?

12 Which big city were *The Out-of-Towners* (1970/1999) visiting and why?

13 To which country were the Royal Cumbrian regiment sent to fight in the 2002 remake of *The Four Feathers*?

14 What was the name of the 1998 remake of the Hitchcock thriller *Dial M For Murder* (1954)?

15 In the 1998 version of *The Parent Trap*, the roles of the meddlesome twin sisters were both played by Lindsay Lohan. Who played the parts in the 1961 Walt Disney original?

And finally . . .

If she was a schoolteacher hired to tutor his children, of which country was he the king?

18　THE PLOT THICKENS

Read what happened and then identify which film it all happened in.

1　A Vietnam war veteran is sent on a covert mission into the Soviet Union to steal the prototype of a revolutionary new jet fighter.

2　A group of eccentric competitors participate in a crazy cross-country car race.

3　A gunslinger-for-hire finds himself in the middle of a war between the Irish and Italian mafia in a prohibition era ghost town.

4　A private detective must find and protect a Buddhist mystic who has been kidnapped by an evil sorcerer.

5　A group of brave chickens attempt to escape their miserable battery-farm existence before the evil farmer's wife can use them as the ingredients in her new pie-making business.

6　A 73-year-old man makes a 6-week journey across America on a lawn-mower.

7　A high school English teacher is outed as a gay man by a former student while accepting an Academy Award. Chaos ensues in the teacher's private life and in the small conservative town where he lives.

8　A clueless male model is brainwashed into killing the Prime Minister of Malaysia.

9　Three divorcees seek revenge on the husbands who left them for younger women.

10　A sexy comic-strip character seduces her creator in order to cross over into the real world.

11　In 1855 a gang of thieves carry out the first ever robbery from a moving train by stealing a payroll of gold bars destined for the Crimea.

12　A couple of maverick pilots fly missions for a secret CIA backed airline during the early days of the Vietnam War.

13　A Nazi hunter discovers a sinister and bizarre plot to rekindle the Third Reich in Paraguay.

14 A man searches for his missing girlfriend after she disappears at a gas station.

15 A smart-ass kid hacks into a top-secret military computer system and inadvertently starts the countdown to World War III.

16 An adventurous little clownfish is snatched from his idyllic coral reef home and forcibly relocated to a fish tank in a dentist's waiting room. His father then begins a frantic search for his kidnapped son.

17 In 1921, a mercurial genius of German expressionist cinema casts a genuine 300-year-old vampire as the lead in his screen adaptation of Bram Stoker's *Dracula*, promising him the neck of the leading lady after filming has wrapped in lieu of any wages.

18 An American lawyer on a business trip to China is falsely accused of murder.

19 A simple fifty-something gardener climbs the social ladder to become a presidential candidate.

20 A group of National Guardsmen on a weekend training exercise in the remote Louisiana swamplands must fight for their lives after they anger the local Cajun community by stealing their canoes.

21 Neighbourhood kids recount the story of five sisters who all committed suicide during their youth 25 years ago.

22 Two FBI agents arrive in a small southern town to investigate the murders of civil rights activists.

23 A group of middle-aged women pose nude for a calendar in order to raise money for charity.

24 An eccentric inventor drags his family to Central America to build an ice factory in the jungle.

25 A retiring police chief makes a promise to the grieving parents of a murdered girl, to catch her killer.

26 In 1876 a US Cavalry officer is seconded to the Japanese army as a military adviser to help train the Emperor's troops in their on-going war against the Samurai warriors. However, after being injured in battle and subsequently taken prisoner by the Samurai, he learns of their code of honour and starts to question his own loyalties.

27 A group of kids sing and dance their way through classes at the New York City High School for the Performing Arts.

28 An Allied and German POW in an Irish internment camp during World War II fight for the love of the same woman.

29 A bored middle-aged Liverpool housewife travels to the Greek Islands to escape the drudgery of her everyday life.

30 'The Daywalker' kicks vampire ass . . . again!

19 MIX UP

Match up **COLUMN 1** to the correct answer in **COLUMN 2**

COLUMN 1   **COLUMN 2**

1 URBAN LEGENDS
   Match the stalk and slash heroes to the correct series of films.

1) Jason Voorhees   1) *Halloween* (1978–2002)
2) Michael Myers   2) *Hellraiser* (1987–2004)
3) Freddy Krueger   3) *Candyman* (1992–99)
4) Daniel Robitaille   4) *A Nightmare on Elm Street*
                              (1984–2003)
5) Pinhead   5) *Friday 13th* (1980–2003)

2 BATMAN'S ARCH-ENEMIES
   Which big name played which particular villainous foe of the Caped
   Crusader?

1) Arnold Schwarzenegger   1) The Riddler
2) Uma Thurman   2) Catwoman
3) Jim Carrey   3) Two-Face
4) Tommy Lee Jones   4) The Penguin
5) Jack Nicholson   5) The Joker
6) Danny DeVito   6) Mr Freeze
7) Michelle Pfeiffer   7) Poison Ivy

… and which 3 actors have played the part of Batman?

3 ALL THINGS SPORTY
   Match the film to its sporty theme.

1) *North Dallas Forty* (1979)   1) Basketball
2) *Angels in the Outfield* (1994) 2) Cycling

3)	*Tin Cup* (1996)	3)	Ice Skating
4)	*Celtic Pride* (1996)	4)	Baseball
5)	*American Flyers* (1985)	5)	American Football
6)	*The Cutting Edge* (1992)	6)	Golf
7)	*Players* (1979)	7)	Tennis

4 MERYL'S ACCENTS
In which film did Meryl Streep use which accent?

1)	Danish	1)	*A Cry in the Dark* (1988)
2)	Australian	2)	*Out of Africa* (1985)
3)	Polish	3)	*Sophie's Choice* (1982)
4)	English	4)	*Plenty* (1985)
5)	Irish	5)	*Dancing at Lughnasa* (1998)
6)	American (her own voice)	6)	*Still of the Night* (1982)

5 PARTNERS IN CRIME
Match up the partners in crime and then identify which film they appeared in together.

1)	Arnold Schwarzenegger	1)	Kurt Russell	....
2)	Al Pacino	2)	James Belushi	....
3)	Sylvester Stallone	3)	John Goodman	....
4)	Robert Duvall	4)	Mark Wahlberg	....
5)	Chow Yun-Fat	5)	Gregory Hines	....
6)	Billy Crystal	6)	Sean Penn	....

6 OH WHAT A LOVELY WAR
... but which one?

1)	*Ride with the Devil* (1999)	1)	Vietnam
2)	*Hamburger Hill* (1987)	2)	World War II

3) *Paradise Road* (1997)
4) *Revolution* (1985)
5) *Three Kings* (1999)
6) *In Love and War* (1996)

3) American War of Independence
4) The Gulf War
5) World War I
6) American Civil War

7 MONSTERS EVERYWHERE
Where were those pesky critters hiding?

1) A cruise ship
2) Chicago's Natural History Museum
3) An abandoned Russian research ship
4) New York's subway system
5) A desolate planet

1) *Deep Rising* (1998)
2) *The Relic* (1997)
3) *Mimic* (1997)
4) *Virus* (1999)
5) *Pitch Black* (2000)

8 FRIENDS
The *Friends* (1994–2004) TV series was so successful that it allowed the previously unknown cast to try their luck on the big screen – some more successfully than others. Match the 'friend' to their big screen appearance.

1) Jennifer Aniston (Rachel)
2) Courtney Cox (Monica)
3) Matt LeBlanc (Joey)
4) Matthew Perry (Chandler)
5) Lisa Kudrow (Phoebe)
6) David Schwimmer (Ross)

1) *The Runner* (1999)
2) *Lost in Space* (1998)
3) *The Pallbearer* (1996)
4) *Picture Perfect* (1997)
5) *Lucky Numbers* (2000)
6) *Fools Rush In* (1997)

9 KARAOKE MOMENTS
Which films were famous for which songs ... however badly sung?

1)	'Say a Little Prayer' – Dionne Warwick	1)	*Beautiful Girls* (1996)
2)	'Sweet Caroline' – Neil Diamond	2)	*A Life Less Ordinary* (1997)
3)	'You've Lost That Loving Feeling' – The Righteous Brothers	3)	*The Deer Hunter* (1978)
4)	'Can't Take my Eyes off of You' – Andy Williams	4)	*Top Gun* (1986)
5)	'Under the Sea' – Bobby Darin	5)	*My Best Friend's Wedding* (1997)

10 SPOILERS
Match the 'twist in the story' to the particular film. (Hey! Everyone must have seen these films by now.)

1)	She was a guy	1)	*The Usual Suspects* (1995)
2)	Maybe he was or wasn't a robot	2)	*Blade Runner* (1982)
3)	He was the Russian spy	3)	*Seven* (1995)
4)	It was all bullshit	4)	*No Way Out* (1987)
5)	His wife's head was in the box	5)	*The Crying Game* (1992)

11 TV BEGINNINGS
Everyone has to start somewhere – even these guys! Match up today's movie stars with yesterday's TV shows on which they achieved their fame and fortune.

1)	Johnny Depp	1)	*ER* (1994–)
2)	Michael J. Fox	2)	*Magnum PI* (1980–88)
3)	David Caruso	3)	*Miami Vice* (1984–89)
4)	Ted Danson	4)	*21 Jump Street* (1987–92)
5)	Don Johnson	5)	*NYPD Blue* (1993–)

6) George Clooney
7) Tom Selleck

6) *Cheers* (1982–93)
7) *Family Ties* (1982–89)

12 GOOD vs. EVIL
Who was fighting who?

1) Spider-Man in *Spider-Man* (2002)
2) Daredevil in *Daredevil* (2003)
3) Flash Gordon in *Flash Gordon* (1980)
4) Supergirl in *Supergirl* (1984)
5) Superman in *Superman II* (1980)
6) He-Man in *Masters of the Universe* (1987)

1) Bullseye
2) General Zod
3) The Green Goblin
4) Skeletor
5) Selena
6) Ming the Merciless

13 TEACHERS
Who was teaching what?

1) Robin Williams in *Dead Poets Society* (1989)
2) Richard Dreyfuss in *Mr Holland's Opus* (1995)
3) Kevin Kline in *The Emperor's Club* (2002)
4) Goldie Hawn in *Wildcats* (1986)
5) Jeff Bridges in *The Mirror Has Two Faces* (1996)

1) Football
2) English
3) Maths
4) History
5) Music

14 TITLE CHANGES
Match the original US film title to how it was retitled for its UK release.

1)	*Off Limits* (1988)	1)	*Léon*
2)	*Diggstown* (1992)	2)	*Saigon*
3)	*Beyond the Limit* (1983)	3)	*Stolen Hearts*
4)	*The Professional* (1994)	4)	*Midnight Sting*
5)	*Two if by Sea* (1996)	5)	*The Honorary Consul*

15 OLD STALWARTS
Who played these old screen favourites and in which films?

1)	Dracula	1)	Christopher Plummer	....
2)	Sherlock Holmes	2)	Gary Oldman	....
3)	God	3)	Christopher Lambert	....
4)	Tarzan	4)	Morgan Freeman	....
5)	Robin Hood	5)	Cary Elwes	....

16 CLICHES
Who played these movie clichés and in which films?

1)	The Innocent Man wrongly imprisoned	1)	Colin Farrell	....
2)	The New Recruit	2)	Kenneth Branagh	....
3)	The OTT Bad Guy	3)	Tom Selleck	....
4)	The 'Fish out of Water'	4)	Edward Norton	....
5)	One man's fight against the odds	5)	Harry Connick Jr	....
6)	The Psycho	6)	Bill Murray	....
7)	The Serial Killer	7)	Cuba Gooding Jr	....

17 FURRY FRIENDS
Who was what? (furry or otherwise)

1)	Dunston	1)	Horse
2)	Paulie	2)	Parrot
3)	Andre	3)	Dog
4)	Spirit	4)	Seal
5)	Cujo	5)	Orang-Utan
6)	Joe Young	6)	Gorilla
7)	Tarka	7)	Otter

18 BOOKWORMS
Match the film to the best-selling author on whose book the screen-play was based.

1)	*Patriot Games* (1992)	1)	Robert Ludlum
2)	*Rising Sun* (1993)	2)	John Grisham
3)	*Dreamcatcher* (2003)	3)	Tom Clancey
4)	*The Osterman Weekend* (1983)	4)	Michael Crichton
5)	*A Time to Kill* (1996)	5)	Stephen King
6)	*The World According to Garp* (1982)	6)	John Irving
7)	*Blood Work* (2002)	7)	Michael Connelly

19 THE BARD
An old screen favourite. Who played which particular Shakespearean character?

1)	*Richard III* (1995)	1)	Kenneth Branagh
2)	*Hamlet* (1996)	2)	Anthony Hopkins
3)	*Henry V* (1989)	3)	Mel Gibson
4)	*Hamlet* (1990)	4)	Kenneth Branagh
5)	*Titus* (1999)	5)	Ian McKellen

20 NEW YORK, NEW YORK
Identify which 'Big Apple' sights were particularly relevant to which films.

1) *Ransom* (1996)
Where the little boy was kidnapped

1) Brooklyn Bridge

2) *Godzilla* (1998)
Where she laid her eggs

2) Empire State Building

3) *Men in Black* (1997)
A first encounter with an alien

3) U.N. Building

4) *The Peacemaker* (1997)
Where the bomb was to go off

4) Guggenheim Museum

5) *Sleepless in Seattle* (1993)
Where Sam and Annie finally meet

5) Madison Square Garden

6) *Kate and Leopold* (2001)
From where time travel was possible

6) Central Park

20 THE NAME GAME 2 – THE DEFINITE ARTICLE

Who played the title role in the following films?

1   *The Wedding Singer* (1998)
2   *The Astronaut's Wife* (1999)
3   *The Horse Whisperer* (1998)
4   *The Postman* (1997)
5   *The French Lieutenant's Woman* (1981)
6   *The Pianist* (2002)
7   *The Man Who Knew Too Little* (1997)
8   *The Rookie* (1990)
9   *The Princess Bride* (1987)
10 *The Bachelor* (1999)
11 *The Distinguished Gentleman* (1992)
12 *The Great Santini* (1979)
13 *The Jerk* (1979)
14 *The Cheap Detective* (1978)
15 *The Limey* (1999)
16 *The Ambassador* (1984)
17 *The Aviator* (1985)
18 *The Toy* (1982)
19 *The Hurricane* (1999)
20 *The One* (2001)
21 *The Babe* (1992)
22 *The Specialist* (1994)
23 *The Contender* (2000)
24 *The Phantom* (1996)
25 *The Man Who Loved Women* (1983)
26 *The Hitcher* (1986)
27 *The Temp* (1993)
28 *The Apostle* (1997)
29 *The Wicked Lady* (1983)
30 *The Tailor of Panama* (2001)

21 WHERE WAS WHERE

21.1 – HOLLYWOOD ABROAD

Which COUNTRY was the backdrop to these films?

1 *The Year of Living Dangerously* (1982)
2 *Ronin* (1998)
3 *Heat and Dust* (1983)
4 *Local Hero* (1983)
5 *Into the West* (1992)
6 *Cry Freedom* (1987)
7 *Up at the Villa* (2000)
8 *City of Joy* (1992)
9 *Before Sunrise* (1995)
10 *High Season* (1987)

21.2 – BRIGHT LIGHTS, BIG CITY

Which US CITY provided the backdrop for these films?

1 *Avalon* (1990)
2 *Nine Months* (1995)
3 *Short Cuts* (1993)
4 *Someone to Watch Over Me* (1987)
5 *Narc* (2002)
6 *Showgirls* (1995)
7 *The Mean Season* (1985)
8 *Striking Distance* (1993)
9 *The Big Easy* (1987)
10 *Blown Away* (1994)

21.3 – ONLY IN THE MOVIES

In which films will you find these ...

TOWNS

1 Seahaven
2 Kingston Falls
3 Duloc
4 Christmas Town
5 Whoville
6 Antonio Bay
7 Champion City
8 San Angeles
9 Holly Springs
10 Perfection

THINGS AND PLACES

11 Rydell High
12 The Corny Collins Dance Show
13 The Bunker Hill Military Academy
14 The Merlin–Flemmer Building
15 Wakefield Prison
16 The Sad Café
17 USS *Alabama*
18 East Palo Alto High School
19 The ancient city of Hamunaptra
20 Spooky Island
21 Mon Signor Hotel
22 The Titty Twister Bar
23 Mayfield Place

24 Nakatomi Plaza
25 Camp Crystal Lake
26 Club Obi-Wan
27 *The Hermann Goering Workout Book*
28 SS *Essess*
29 The *Antonia Graza*
30 The Claymoore Psychiatric Hospital

22 DEBUTS

22.1 – OUT FRONT

Which ACTORS made their big screen debuts in these films?

1 *Heavenly Creatures* (1994)
2 *48 Hrs.* (1982)
3 *Carbon Copy* (1981)
4 *Altered States* (1980)
5 *Kuffs* (1992)
6 *Rich and Famous* (1981)
7 *Jungle Fever* (1991)
8 *Eyes of a Stranger* (1981)
9 *Lucas* (1986)
10 *The Tall Guy* (1989)

22.2 – BEHIND THE CAMERA

Which DIRECTORS began their careers with these films?

1 *Truly Madly Deeply* (1991)
2 *Boyz N the Hood* (1991)
3 *This Is My Life* (1992)
4 *Diner* (1982)
5 *Scandal* (1989)
6 *Shallow Grave* (1994)
7 *Con Air* (1997)
8 *Kill Me Again* (1989)
9 *Clerks* (1994)
10 *Speed* (1994)

22.3 – REVERSAL OF FORTUNE

Which ACTORS made their DIRECTORAL DEBUTS with these films?

1   *The Man Without a Face* (1993)
2   *A Bronx Tale* (1993)
3   *Keeping the Faith* (2000)
4   *Albino Alligator* (1996)
5   *Little Man Tate* (1991)
6   *Bob Roberts* (1992)
7   *Bopha!* (1993)
8   *Wisdom* (1986)
9   *August* (1996)
10 *Mac* (1992)

??? 23 THE FILMOGRAPHY

23.1 – THE C.V.

Which actor has played all these roles?

1 A Polish baker
A gay nightclub owner
A Cadillac salesman
An eccentric toy maker
Popeye

2 A Russian submarine captain
An immortal Spanish swordsman
A Franciscan monk (turned amateur detective)
A reclusive Pulitzer Prize-winning author
King Arthur

3 The Station Manager of KGAB Radio
A fake cop
A fashion photographer
A rich playboy
The Shadow

4 A stand-up comedian
A Peace Corp. worker
A prison guard
A baseball coach
Sheriff Woody

5 A maverick car designer
A suicidal radio DJ
An alien

An air-crash survivor
'Wild' Bill Hickok

6 A 'Pink Lady'
A lounge singer
A TV newsreader
A Dallas housewife
Queen of the Fairies

7 A former Olympic boxer
A Catholic priest
A gang leader
T.S. Eliot
Jesus of Nazareth

8 An insurance investigator
A 'small-time' crook
A kosher butcher
A human chameleon
Z-4195

9 A successful advertising executive
A vampire
'The Chosen One'
An African prince
A donkey

10 A sleazy boxing promoter
A dead-end talent scout
A college English professor
A corrupt oil company owner
Sherlock Holmes

23.2 – THE THREESOME

Identify the actor from a shortlist of three films.

1 *Chain Reaction* (1996), *Kiss the Girls* (1997), *High Crimes* (2002)
2 *Sweet and Lowdown* (1999), *Vatel* (2000), *Chelsea Walls* (2001)
3 *The Baby of Macon* (1993), *Strange Days* (1995), *The End of the Affair* (1999)
4 *Born Yesterday* (1993), *Two Much* (1996), *Another Day in Paradise* (1998)
5 *When a Man Loves a Woman* (1994), *Night Falls on Manhattan* (1997), *Just the Ticket* (1999)
6 *My Stepmother is an Alien* (1988), *The Real McCoy* (1993), *I Dreamed of Africa* (2000)
7 *Siesta* (1987), *Switch* (1991), *Mercy* (2000)
8 *I Love You to Death* (1990), *The Doctor* (1991), *Second Best* (1994)
9 *The House on Carroll Street* (1988), *Arachnophobia* (1990), *Welcome Home, Roxy Carmichael* (1990)
10 *A River Runs Through It* (1992), *Sleepers* (1996), *Spy Game* (2001)

23.3 – THE ONE

Identify the film.

1 The one where Arnie gets pregnant.
2 The one with Bill and the elephant.
3 The one where Mr Hoffman does battle with a big mysterious round thing from outer space.
4 The one where Bette is kidnapped by Huey and Duey.
5 The one where Mel's fighting the English . . . again!
6 The one where Billy Bob finds a bag full of money.

7   The one where Jack howls at the moon.
8   The one where Goldie joins the army.
9   The one with Jen and the big snake.
10 The one where Clint sings country.
11 The one with Sammy L. in a kilt.
12 The one with Bruce in a pink bunny suit.
13 The one with Gwynnie in a 350lb fat suit.
14 The one with Bren stuck in a nuclear bunker for 35 years.
15 The one where Whoopi coaches the New York Knicks.

23.4 – THE OBSCURE

Sometimes a film just fades away into obscurity; never to appear on DVD, unlikely even to be seen on TV. This is usually because the film stinks, and it is difficult to find an exception to this rule amongst the forgotten 'gems' listed below. How well do you remember these misunderstood classics of the silver screen? Just name the title of the film.

1   That one with John Goodman as the unlikely next King of England.
2   That one with Tom Selleck as a gentleman thief in 1930s London.
3   That one with David Warner, as Jack The Ripper, who steals H.G. Wells' time machine and travels to 1970s San Francisco. In a city and time where murders were commonplace, he remarked – 'In 1893 I was a freak. Today, I'm an amateur.'
4   That one where Paul McCartney plays himself searching for some stolen master tapes of his latest songs.
5   That one about a man reincarnated as a dog so he can find his murderer. Chevy Chase was the voice of the sleuthing mutt.
6   That one with Anthony Quinn as a Libyan resistance fighter leading a rebellion against Rod Steiger and his occupying army.

7 That one with Charlton Heston as an archaeologist who discovers that his daughter is possessed by the spirit of an evil queen. Much ancient Egyptian mumbo jumbo followed.

8 That old Blake Edwards comedy, famous for a topless Julie Andrews ... and that's about all.

9 Julie Andrews again. This time she keeps her clothes on, suffers from a crippling disease and plays the violin a lot.

10 That one with David Carradine hunting down a giant flying lizard terrorising the good folks of the Big Apple.

Whilst researching possible entries in this section, it soon became apparent that almost every Burt Reynolds film made during the last 25 years could easily qualify for inclusion as an obscure and forgotten 'classic'. The temptation to give Burt a little section all to himself was just too hard to resist.

11 The one with Burt as a jewel thief and David Niven as the detective on his trail.

12 The one with Burt as an ageing stuntman.

13 The one where Burt is a playboy bachelor searching for the perfect woman to have his baby.

14 The one where Burt is the tough, fearless, lone-wolf type of cop partnered with ... an 8-year-old kid.

15 The one with Burt as a cop (again!) and Liza Minnelli as a call-girl.

23.5 – THE GAPS

Complete the gaps in the filmography.

1 GEENA DAVIS
   Hero (1992), *Angie* (1994), *Speechless* (1994), ...
   (1995), *The Long Kiss Goodnight* (1996)

   Clue: Pirates

2 NICOLE KIDMAN
   Eyes Wide Shut (1999), *Moulin Rouge* (2001), ...
   (2001), *Birthday Girl* (2001), *The Hours* (2002)

   Clue: Haunted houses

3 LAURENCE FISHBURNE
   Higher Learning (1995), *Bad Company* (1995), *Just Cause* (1995),
   . . . . (1995), *Fled* (1996)

   Clue: Shakespeare

4 NICK NOLTE
   Q & A (1990), *Cape Fear* (1991), *The Prince of Tides* (1991),
   . . . . (1992), *I'll Do Anything* (1994)

   Clue: Miracle cures

5 GENE HACKMAN
   All Night Long (1981), ... (1983), *Uncommon Valor*
   (1983), *Misunderstood* (1984), *Twice in a Lifetime* (1985)

   Clue: Nicaragua

6 SUSAN SARANDON
The Client (1994), *Little Women* (1994), *Safe Passage* (1994),
.... (1995), *Twilight* (1998)

Clue: Death Row

7 BILL MURRAY
Little Shop of Horrors (1986), *Scrooged* (1988), *Ghostbusters II*
(1989), ... (1990), *What About Bob?* (1991)

Clue: Clowns

8 TOM CRUISE
All the Right Moves (1983), *Legend* (1985), *Top Gun* (1986), *The Color
of Money* (1986), ... (1988)

Clue: Exotic drinks

9 JESSICA LANGE
Night and the City (1992), *Blue Sky* (1994), *Losing Isaiah* (1995),
.... (1995), *A Thousand Acres* (1997)

Clue: Scotland

10 DEBRA WINGER
Mike's Murder (1984), *Legal Eagles* (1986), ...
(1987), *Betrayed* (1988), *Everybody Wins* (1990)

Clue: Spiders

23.6 – THE END BIT

Was the film one of theirs? Yes or No?

1 Winona Ryder: *Heathers* (1989)
2 Sigourney Weaver: *Half Moon Street* (1986)
3 Tim Roth: *Little Odessa* (1994)
4 Peter O'Toole: *The Stunt Man* (1980)
5 Neve Campbell: *A Guy Thing* (2003)
6 Mira Sorvino: *The Replacement Killers* (1998)
7 Mary Louise Parker: *Miami Rhapsody* (1995)
8 Natasha Richardson: *Loch Ness* (1996)
9 Richard Harris: *The Field* (1990)
10 Linda Fiorentino: *The Last Seduction* (1994)
11 Kate Beckinsale: *Laurel Canyon* (2002)
12 Kate Winslet: *The Wings Of The Dove* (1997)
13 Catherine Zeta-Jones: *The Haunting* (1999)
14 Ashley Judd: *Congo* (1995)
15 Reese Witherspoon: *Simply Irresistible* (1999)
16 Tom Berenger: *Sniper* (1993)
17 Heath Ledger: *Ned Kelly* (2003)
18 Liam Neeson: *In the Name of the Father* (1993)
19 Ed Harris: *Personal Best* (1982)
20 Colin Farrell: *Hart's War* (2002)

24.1 – NAMING NAMES

Identify which actors played these famous characters and in which films?

1 Jack Slater
2 Joan Wilder
3 Wayne Campbell
4 Seth Brundle
5 Castor Troy
6 Xander Cage
7 Isaac Davis
8 Corrina Washington
9 Ace Ventura
10 William Munny
11 Roy Hobbs
12 Jimmy Alto
13 Daniel Hillard
14 Suzy Diamond
15 Mrs Flax

16 Buddy Rydell
17 Cher Horowitz
18 Paul Sheldon
19 Sidney Prescott
20 Michael Hfuhruhurr
21 Alex Forrest
22 Martin Blank
23 Paul Kersey
24 Marge Gunderson
25 Carlito Brigante
26 Rupert Pupkin
27 Gilbert Grape
28 Lara Croft
29 Elwood Blues
30 Simon Templar

24.2 – THE PERSONALITIES

Identify the character name, actor and the film from this short description.

1 Respectable psychiatrist by day; knife-wielding transvestite killer by night.
2 A feisty young Mexican lass; sword fighter and tango dancer.
3 A clean-cut American playboy living the sun-kissed high life in 1930s Italy.
4 Shy school kid by day; 'shock jock' DJ by night.
5 A teenage roller-skating starlet of 1970s porn films.

6 Steel worker by day; exotic dancer by night.

7 Successful Wall Street businessman by day; mad, unstoppable, serial killer by night.

8 A bakery worker with a love of opera, life ... and his brother's fiancée.

9 A successful TV producer and game show host in his public life; a globe-trotting CIA assassin in his private life.

10 A lawyer by day and an acrobatic martial arts superhero by night.

24.3 – IT'S A LIVING

How did these guys earn their living?

1 Michael Douglas in *The Star Chamber* (1983)

2 John Travolta in *Domestic Disturbance* (2001)

3 Alan Alda in *The Seduction of Joe Tynan* (1979)

4 Richard Gere in *Primal Fear* (1996)

5 Tom Berenger in *Shattered* (1991)

6 Emilio Estevez in *Men at Work* (1990)

7 Dennis Quaid in *Frequency* (2000)

8 James Garner in *Murphy's Romance* (1985)

9 Rebecca De Mornay in *Risky Business* (1983)

10 Tobey Maguire in *Seabiscuit* (2003)

24.4 – THE VOICE TALENT

With all things animated enjoying a resurgence in popularity in recent years, it's no wonder that Hollywood's great and good are falling over themselves for a chance to lend their voices to the latest cuddly cartoon creations to hit the silver screen. So, who exactly was the 'voice talent' behind these well-known characters?

1 Balto in *Balto* (1995)
2 Princess Fiona in *Shrek* (2001–04)
3 Anastasia in *Anastasia* (1997)
4 Jessie in *Toy Story 2* (1999)
5 The Blue Genie of the Lamp in *Aladdin* (1992)
6 Esmeralda in *The Hunchback of Notre Dame* (1996)
7 Simba in *The Lion King* (1994)
8 Jane in *Tarzan* (1999)
9 Mushu in *Mulan* (1998)
10 Moses in *The Prince of Egypt* (1998)

24.5 – THE BACK CATALOGUE

Sometimes an actor doesn't just play *one* memorable character in their career ... they play quite a few of them. Who played all these famous names?

1 Tony Manero, Gabriel Shear, Chili Palmer and Danny Zuko.
2 Ethan Hunt, Mitch McDeere, Ron Kovic and Lestat de Lioncourt.
3 Vivian Ward, Mary Reilly, Darby Shaw and Katherine Watson.
4 Henry Turner, Jack Trainer, Joe Gavilan and Richard Kimble.
5 Crash Davis, Frank Farmer, Jim Garrison and Charley Waite.
6 Dixie Dwyer, Edward Lewis, Zack Mayo and Julian Kaye.
7 Billy Ray Valentine, Reggie Hammond, Axel Foley and Sherman Klump.

24.6 – THE CAST LIST

Which films featured all these character names in its cast?

1 Turkish, Brick Top Polford, Mickey O'Neil, Bullet Tooth Tony, Franky Four Fingers, Mullet and Boris 'The Blade' Yurinov.
2 Big Boy Caprice, Breathless Mahoney, Flattop, Pruneface, Numbers, 88 Keys and Mumbles.
3 Noodles, Max, Cockeye, Patsy, Deborah, Carol and Fat Moe.
4 Jim, Nadia, Michelle, Stifler, Finch, Kevin, Vicky, Oz, Jessica, Heather and Jim's Dad.
5 Robin Hood, King Agamemnon, Pansy, Napoleon, Vincent, Supreme Being and Winston The Ogre.
6 The Bride (*aka* Black Mamba), Bill, Elle Driver (*aka* California Mountain Snake), Budd (*aka* Sidewinder), Vernita Green (*aka* Copperhead), O-Ren Ishi (*aka* Cottonmouth), Crazy 88 Fighter, Go Go Yubari and Johnny Mo.
7 Allan Quatermain, Captain Nemo, Dorian Gray, Tom Sawyer, Mina Harker, The Invisible Man, Dr Jekyll and Mr Hyde, M, Dante, Sanderson Reed and Nigel.
8 Mikey, Brand, Chunk, Mouth, Andy, Stef, Data and Sloth.
9 Dallas, Ripley, Lambert, Brett, Kane, Ash, Parker and Jones the Cat.
10 Kirby, Billy, Kevin, Jules, Alec, Lesley, Wendy and Dale Biberman.

❓❓ 25 5×5

25.1 – THE GIMMICKS

How did the names of these films appear on the posters?

1 *Existenz* (1999)
2 *Seven* (1995)
3 *Jungle to Jungle* (1997)
4 *Thirteen Ghosts* (2001)
5 *Simone* (2002)

25.2 – TWICE AROUND

Hollywood is sometimes like waiting for a bus. You can wait a lifetime for a certain storyline to make it to the big screen and then suddenly two films (virtually identical) come along at the same time! Can you remember the title of the other film released in the same year as those listed below that dealt with exactly the same subject matter.

1 *Mission to Mars* (2000)
   A sci-fi adventure involving an ill-fated voyage to Earth's nearest neighbour.
2 *Antz* (1998)
   A CG animated comedy about those pesky little creatures that invade our homes every summer.
3 *Wyatt Earp* (1994)
   The life and times of the legendary Wild West gunfighter.
4 *Christopher Columbus – The Discovery* (1992)
   The adventures of the famous fifteenth-century Italian explorer.
5 *Fairytale: A True Story* (1997)
   Stories about the existence (or not) of fairies.

25.3 – THE ALTERNATIVE TITLE

What was the full title of the film to which these promotional abbreviations refer?

1 X-2
2 M:i-2
3 LXG
4 ID4
5 MIIB

25.4 – THE COLOUR SCHEME OF THINGS

What colour were they?

1 The CADILLAC
2 The OLEANDER
3 The DAWN
4 The CHIPS
5 The ROBE

25.5 – WHAT MIGHT HAVE BEEN

Can you guess the much snappier version of the movie's title from its literal alternative meaning listed below?

1 Irritability and restlessness caused by living in isolation or a confined space for a prolonged period of time.
2 Third person pronoun serving as the plural of HE, SHE or IT. Often used as the subject of a verb to refer to people, animals or things already mentioned or, more generally, to a group of people not clearly described.
3 An improbable or fanciful story.
4 Something extremely complex or torturous in structure, arrangement, or character.
5 A large, black bird with a loud unpleasant cry.

26 SMART TALK 2

?

A virtual rehash of CHAPTER 8, only this time featuring more than one person with something to say! Identify the films from which these lines of dialogue were taken.

If you're really clever you might want to name the actors and characters too! The character names have obviously been omitted and replaced with As, Bs or Cs, otherwise it would be too easy! Those letters in italics are supporting or 'bit-part' actors and therefore difficult to guess ... maybe?

1 A Ten more seconds, and I'm leaving.
   B What did you say?
   A I said 'Ten more seconds, and I'm leaving'.
   B Oh.
   A Wait, what did you think I said?
   B Earn more sessions by sleeving.

2 A Because of my mistake, six men didn't return from that raid.
   B Seven. Lieutenant Zip died this morning.

3 A There's something I've been meaning to ask you for some time now.
   B What's that?
   A Can you cure me?
   B No. We can care for you, but we can't cure you.

4 A *Look, uh, these people wanna meet you.*
   B What?
   A *They're stand-up guys.*
   B If I wanna meet people, I'll go to a fuckin' country club!

5 A You spear the knife into the bag, then pick some of the drugs up with the knife, then lightly press it on your tongue. And that's how TV cops taste drugs!
B What if it's cyanide?

6 A I expected the Rocky Mountains to be a little rockier than this.
B I was thinking the same thing.
A That John Denver is full of shit, man.

7 A I want to spend the night with you.
B Do you mean sleep over?
A Well . . . yeah!
B Well, OK . . . but I get to be on top!

8 A Would you like to come in?
B I'd rather stick needles in my eyes.

9 *A* *You're not exactly the smartest guy I ever ran across.*
B Oh yeah? And who are you, Alfred Einstein?

10 A What are you doing?
B Adjusting your breasts. You fainted and they shifted all out of whack.

11 A He's leaving, isn't he?
B *Tomorrow morning. He'll need his city clothes.*
A But why? What does he have to go back to?
B *He's going back to his world, where he belongs.*

12 A You a real cowboy?

   B Depends on what you think a real cowboy is?

   A Can you 2-step?

   B Course.

   A Wanna prove it?

13 A Are you saying that nobody in New York will work with me?

   B No, no, that's too limited ... nobody in Hollywood wants to work with you either!

14 A You're going to give her an injection of adrenaline directly to her heart.

   B Then what happens?

   A I'm curious about that myself.

15 A Is this heaven?

   B No, it's Iowa.

16 A Idgie and her friend Ruth ran the Whistle Stop Café. Idgie was a character, all right. But how anybody could have thought she murdered that man is beyond me.

   B I beg your pardon?

17 A This day has been rather disappointing, I don't mind telling you.

   B Why, because you didn't get to kill everybody?

18 A He had always threatened to kill me in public.

   B Why would he want to kill you in public?

   C I think she meant, he threatened in public to kill her.

   B Oh.

19 A I feel great.
  B You wouldn't bullshit me?
  A My God, I'm telling the truth!
  C Why shouldn't he feel good? I feel tremendous! I'm ready to take on the world!

20 A If we don't have to hide my studying from God, then why from the neighbours?
  B *Why? Because I trust God will understand. I'm not so sure about the neighbours.*

27   BODY PARTS 2

27.1 – THE NUMBERS

Find the missing numbers to complete the film title. Is that simple or is that simple?

1 *Bat* ... (1988)
2 *Girl* ... (1996)
3 *... Heads In a Duffel Bag* (1997)
4 *Code* ... (2003)
5 *... Minutes* (2001)
6 *Murder at* ... (1997)
7 *Passenger* ... (1992)
8 *... Million Ways to Die* (1986)
9 *... Cigarettes* (1999)
10 *U -* ... (2000)
11 *... Things I Hate About You* (1999)
12 *Jennifer* ... (1992)
13 *... Days in the Valley* (1996)
14 *Roadhouse* ... (1984)
15 *... Conversations About One Thing* (2001)
16 *Track* ... (1988)
17 *Buffalo* ... (1998)
18 *... Miles to Graceland* (2001)
19 *... AM* (2001)
20 *... Charing Cross Road* (1987)
21 *Love Potion #* ... (1992)
22 *... Pick Up* (1986)
23 *Transylvania* ... (1985)
24 *Article* ... (1992)
25 *Session* ... (2001)

?₀?

27.2 – THE MATHS

Using the answers in THE NUMBERS section on the previous page (for example for question 1 below you need the answers to questions 19 and 11) complete these simple sums to reveal a missing number. From this number and with the help of a little clue, identify the name of another film.

1 $19 + 11$
Clue: Ill-fated space flights

2 $7 - 22 + 19$
Clue: Home movies

3 $4 + 8$
Clue: Missing police cars

4 $20 - 4 - 16 - 13$
Clue: Nazis and The Dalai Lama

5 $17 - 4 - 11$
Clue: Unwanted boyfriends

6 $18/19/11 + 13$
Clue: Lots of dogs . . . again!

7 $1 - 25 - 13$
Clue: The perfect woman

1 *THE SHINING* (1980)
The book that Jack Torrance was writing contained only one line typed over and over again. What was it?

(a) Jack and Jill went up the hill.
(b) All work and no play makes Jack a dull boy.
(c) It's a MAD MAD world.
(d) The insanity of it all.
(e) When Johnny comes marching home again . . .

2 *THE RUNAWAY BRIDE* (1999)
Maggie Carpenter ran from the church, leaving yet another potential husband at the altar. She fled the scene by hitching a ride on a truck belonging to which famous courier company?

(a) UPS
(b) TNT
(c) FedEx
(d) DHL

3 *COOL RUNNINGS* (1993)
The bobsleigh team competing in the Winter Olympics came from which Caribbean island?

(a) Barbados
(b) Trinidad and Tobago
(c) Cuba
(d) Jamaica

4 *MAGNOLIA* (1999)
What fell from the sky during the climactic storm scene?

(a) Frogs

(b) Fish
(c) Maggots
(d) Grasshoppers
(e) Dust

5 *WAG THE DOG* (1997)
Against which country did the USA declare war?

(a) Libya
(b) Mexico
(c) Albania
(d) Japan
(e) Canada

6 *BOWFINGER* (1999)
What was the name of director Bobby Bowfinger's film?

(a) *Skinny Snow*
(b) *Chubby Rain*
(c) *Patchy Fog*
(d) *Whistling Wind*

7 *INDECENT PROPOSAL* (1993)
Exactly what was the price John Gage was willing to pay?

(a) $1,000,000
(b) $100,000 + 'All-You-Can-Eat' at the Casino's buffet
(c) $2,347,960 and 31 cents
(d) $500,000
(e) A Ferrari

8 *LEAVING LAS VEGAS* (1995)
Why did Ben Sanderson go to Las Vegas?

(a) To find his ex-girlfriend
(b) To drink himself to death
(c) To recover a bag of stolen money
(d) To gamble away his family fortune
(e) To kill a man he thinks has double-crossed him

9 *PLEASANTVILLE* (1998)
What was the first thing to change from black and white into colour?

(a) PINK: Bubblegum
(b) RED: Tail-light
(c) YELLOW: Banana
(d) GREEN: Leaf
(e) RED: Rose

10 *AN AMERICAN WEREWOLF IN LONDON* (1981)
What was the name of the Dartmoor pub that the two unlucky American tourists stumbled across?

(a) The Butchered Pig
(b) The Wolf In Sheep's Clothing
(c) The Red Lion
(d) The Slaughtered Lamb
(e) The Slain Goose

11 *APOCALYPSE NOW* (1979)
'I love the smell of Napalm in the morning,' said Lt. Col. William Kilgore. Because it smells like ... ?

(a) Victory
(b) Death

(c) His Zippo lighter

(d) Justice

(e) His father's barbecue

12 *EYES WIDE SHUT* (1999)

What was the password?

(a) Medusa

(b) Fidelio

(c) Lollipop

(d) Turandot

(e) Aida

13 *SIGNS* (2002)

How were Graham Hess and his family able to listen to the Alien 'chatter'?

(a) CB radio

(b) A baby alarm

(c) An old black and white TV set

(d) A cordless phone

(e) The Internet

14 *NOTTING HILL* (1999)

For which publication did Will Thacker pretend to write film reviews?

(a) *Premiere*

(b) *Horse and Hound*

(c) *Harpers and Queen*

(d) *GQ*

(e) *Playboy*

15 *A FISH CALLED WANDA* (1988)
Which language did Archie use to seduce Wanda?

(a) Chinese
(b) Serbo-Croat
(c) Russian
(d) French
(e) Gaelic

16 *BREWSTER'S MILLIONS* (1985)
How did 'Monty' Brewster inherit his full $300m fortune?

(a) By working for a kids' charity for two months
(b) By blowing $30,000,000 in 30 days
(c) By (fair means or foul) being elected chairman of his grand-father's publishing empire
(d) By poisoning his evil twin brother, Nigel
(e) With a toss of a coin

17 *BRIDGET JONES'S DIARY* (2001)
To which Jane Austen novel does this unlikely comedy pay homage?

(a) *Sense and Sensibility*
(b) *Emma*
(c) *Persuasion*
(d) *Pride And Prejudice*
(e) *Northanger Abbey*

18 *THE TERMINATOR* (1984)
Just exactly which model of unstoppable killing machine was the original Terminator?

(a) T-1

(b) T-5
(c) T-800
(d) T-1000
(e) T-42

19 *PHENOMENON* (1996)
Which language was George Malley able to learn in only twenty minutes?

(a) Portuguese
(b) French
(c) German
(d) Spanish
(e) Chinese

20 *FATAL ATTRACTION* (1987)
Which family pet suffered an untimely and premature death?

(a) Hamster
(b) Rabbit
(c) Dog
(d) Cat
(e) Goldfish

29 TWO OF A KIND

Two people. One type. Just decide who it was in the particular film.

1 SERIOUS – Robert De Niro or Al Pacino: *People I Know* (2002)

2 CLOWNS – Robin Williams or Jim Carrey: *Bicentennial Man* (1999)

3 BABIES – Thora Birch or Anna Paquin: *Now and Then* (1995)

4 YOUNGSTERS – Sarah Michelle Gellar or Julia Stiles: *Save The Last Dance* (2001)

5 RISING – Owen Wilson or Tobey Maguire: *The Big Bounce* (2003)

6 FALLING – Kurt Russell or Ray Liotta: *Operation Dumbo Drop* (1995)

7 FORGOTTEN – Sean Young or Kelly McGillis: *Love Crimes* (1992)

8 ALMOST FAMOUS – Bill Paxton or Bill Pullman: *The Last Supper* (1995)

9 CAN DO NO WRONG – Tom Hanks or Tom Cruise: *Bachelor Party* (1984)

10 TOP OF THEIR GAME – Harrison Ford or Mel Gibson: *Six Days Seven Nights* (1998)

11 RESPECT – Gene Hackman or Robert Duvall: *Narrow Margin* (1990)

12 EVERGREEN – Sean Connery or Paul Newman: *Where The Money Is* (2000)

13 LEGENDS – Burt Lancaster or Robert Mitchum: *Atlantic City* (1980)

14 BLONDES – Helen Hunt or Laura Dern: *The Waterdance* (1992)

15 FLUFFY – Sandra Bullock or Meg Ryan: *In the Cut* (2003)

16 SWEET THINGS – Gwyneth Paltrow or Cameron Diaz: *Feeling Minnesota* (1996)

17 WILD THINGS – Drew Barrymore or Angelina Jolie: *Riding in Cars with Boys* (2001)

18 SEXY – Demi Moore or Sharon Stone: *We're No Angels* (1989)

19 DIZZY – Goldie Hawn or Diane Keaton: *Shoot the Moon* (1982)

20 BABES – Penélope Cruz or Jennifer Lopez: *The Hi-Lo Country* (1998)

21 HUNKS – George Clooney or Russell Crowe: *One Fine Day* (1996)

22 ACTION MEN – Steven Seagal or Chuck Norris: *Exit Wounds* (2001)

23 TOUGH GUYS – Bruce Willis or Nick Nolte: *Farewell to the King* (1989)

24 NERDY TYPES – Martin Short or Rick Moranis: *Splitting Heirs* (1993)

25 NAUGHTY BOYS – Christian Slater or Robert Downey Jr: *Heart and Souls* (1993)

26 PRETTY BOYS – Brad Pitt or Leonardo Di Caprio: *The Basketball Diaries* (1995)

27 QUIRKY – Jeff Bridges or Kevin Spacey: *The Big Kahuna* (1999)

28 SLEAZY – Joe Pesci or Steve Buscemi: *Trees Lounge* (1996)

29 WISE-ASS – Bill Murray or Chevy Chase: *Fletch* (1985)

30 OBSCURE – Campbell Scott or Jason Patric: *Rush* (1991)

31 INTELLIGENT – Jeremy Irons or John Malkovich: *Reversal of Fortune* (1990)

32 SLICK – Andy Garcia or Antonio Banderas: *Original Sin* (2001)

33 FUNNY – Ben Stiller or Adam Sandler: *Flirting with Disaster* (1996)

34 UNFUNNY – Chris Rock or Martin Lawrence: *Big Momma's House* (2000)

35 COOL – Samuel L. Jackson or Denzel Washington: *Mo' Better Blues* (1990)

36 WORK SHY – Warren Beatty or Marlon Brando: *A Dry White Season* (1989)

37 WORKAHOLIC – Philip Seymour Hoffman or John C. Reilly: *Flawless* (1999)

38 DIFFICULT – Val Kilmer or . . . not Val Kilmer: *Thunderheart* (1992)

39 CROSSOVER – Madonna or Cher: *Body of Evidence* (1993)

40 OLD GENTLEMEN – David Niven or John Mills: *The Sea Wolves* (1980)

41 OLD DAMES – Katharine Hepburn or Bette Davis: *The Whales of August* (1987)

42 FAMILIAR FACES – J.T. Walsh or Craig T. Nelson: *The Client* (1994)

43 GRISLY – Sam Elliott or Kris Kristofferson: *Mask* (1985)

44 INDEPENDENT – Ed Burns or Eric Stoltz: *Killing Zoe* (1994)

45 STRANGE – Harry Dean Stanton or Dennis Hopper: *Pretty in Pink* (1986)

46 ALL AMERICAN – Chris O'Donnell or Matt Damon: *Circle of Friends* (1995)

47 ICEY – Ice T or Ice Cube: *New Jack City* (1991)

48 CAREER HIGHS – Ben Affleck or Colin Farrell: *SWAT* (2003)

49 CAREER DOLDRUMS – Burt Reynolds or Ryan O'Neal: *So Fine* (1981)

50 FROM BAD TO WORSE – Steve Guttenberg or Judge Reinhold: *High Spirits* (1988)

51 WORST – Charlie Sheen or Rob Lowe: *Navy SEALS* (1990)

52 ONE HIT – Alicia Silverstone or Mira Sorvino: *Excess Baggage* (1997)

53 ITALIAN – Chazz Palminteri or Stanley Tucci: *Bullets Over Broadway* (1994)

54 IRISH – Liam Neeson or Gabriel Byrne: *Leap of Faith* (1992)

55 LORDS – Laurence Olivier or John Gielgud: *Prospero's Books* (1991)

56 BROTHERS – Ralph Fiennes or Joseph Fiennes: *Spider* (2002)

57 SISTERS – Rosanna Arquette or Patricia Arquette: *Beyond Rangoon* (1995)

58 VILLAINS – Christopher Walken or Gary Oldman: *Nick of Time* (1995)

59 SHOWBIZ – Liza Minnelli or Barbra Streisand: *Stepping Out* (1991)

60 CHALK AND CHEESE – John Candy or Danny DeVito: *Who's Harry Crumb?* (1989)

? **30 JAMES BOND**

'You appear with the tedious inevitability of an unloved season, Mr Bond,' said Hugo Drax. This is true, but the world would be a much scarier place without him.

1 Who wrote the original novels on which the films are based?
2 How many 'official' films later?
3 Which six actors have played the part of the famous secret agent?
4 Which of those famous six played the role in these films?
   (a) *A View to a Kill*
   (b) *Die Another Day*
   (c) *You Only Live Twice*
   (d) *Dr No*
   (e) *For Your Eyes Only*
5 In which film does 007 get married?
6 *Never Say Never Again* (1983) was little more than an 'unofficial' remake of which earlier 'official' 007 film?
7 In which film does James Bond have his 'licence to kill' revoked?
8 Just exactly what does S.P.E.C.T.R.E. mean?
9 Which is the only Bond flick to have won an Oscar?
10 How many seconds were left on the clock when 007 finally defused Mr Goldfinger's bomb?
11 Who or what was Little Nellie?
12 Sometimes he can be such a smart-ass! In which film did 007 demonstrate his ability to distinguish the vintage of wine that a particular sherry is based on?
13 Who played the evil arms dealer Brad Whitaker in *The Living Daylights* (1987) but then later went on to play Bond's CIA chum Jack Wade in *GoldenEye* (1995) and *Tomorrow Never Dies* (1997)?
14 Who is the only person to have sung over the opening credits more than once?

15 In which film did 007 swap his usual expensive sports car for a beat-up old Citroën 2CV?

16 What was 007 dressed as to defuse a bomb in the climactic scene of *Octopussy* (1983)?

    (a)   A circus clown

    (b)   A gorilla

    (c)   Charlie Chaplin

    (d)   A teddy bear

17 What was so special about the Lotus Esprit in *The Spy Who Loved Me* (1977)?

18 Which of the following Bond girls didn't succumb to 007's charms?

    (a)   Pussy Galore in *Goldfinger* (1964)

    (b)   Plenty O'Toole in *Diamonds Are Forever* (1971)

    (c)   May Day in *A View to a Kill* (1985)

    (d)   Solitaire in *Live and Let Die* (1973)

19 In which film did 007 remark that drinking Dom Perignon at the wrong temperature was 'like listening to The Beatles without ear-muffs'?

20 What was Q's real name?

21 Who said it and in which film?

    (a)   'The pleasure of the kill is in the chase.'

    (b)   'Look after Mr Bond. See that some harm comes to him.'

    (c)   'The distance between insanity and genius is measured only by success.'

22 Sometimes even the world's least-secret secret agent uses an alias to get the job done. In which films did 007 use the following false names?

    (a)   James St. John Smyth

    (b)   David Somerset

    (c)   Robert Sterling

23 Who was Felix Leiter and how did he die?

24 In which films did the following bad-guys appear?
   (a) Mr Kid and Mr Wint
   (b) Jaws
   (c) Nick Nack
   (d) Odd Job
   (e) Tee Hee

And which one of them found true love with a little blonde lady called Dolly?

25 What was the name of the bogus company used by MI6 as a 'front' to conceal their true identity?

And finally . . .

Only one James Bond film has not yet been mentioned in either a question or an answer. Which is it?

31 BITS AND PIECES

A mishmash of bits and pieces that don't fit anywhere else in particular.

1 Who were 'The world's hardest working band'?

2 *Ever After* (1998) was a reworking of which famous fairy tale?

3 In which two completely unrelated films has Michael Keaton played the same character of FBI agent Ray Nicolette?

4 In which medieval tale does a mouse try to reunite a wolf and a hawk in love?

5 If Jessica Lange was the foster mother, who was the real mother?

6 Which company had as its motto: 'We scare because we care'?

7 Which very recent film jokingly included the credit ' . . . and introducing Julia Roberts'?

8 Which old crooner made his last big screen appearance in a starring role in *The First Deadly Sin* (1980)?

9 In which film did the 'Singing Bush' appear?

10 What was the nickname for the small New Jersey town of Garrison?

11 Which 1994 musical was so bad that when it was finally released in the theatres, it was no longer a musical – all the songs having been removed?

12 Which English Dame has played the part of which two English monarchs in which two films?

13 Amy Irving was credited with Jessica Rabbit's singing voice in *Who Framed Roger Rabbit?* (1988), but who was uncredited with her speaking voice?

14 Who is Ray DiTutto and in which film was he the *King of the Moon*?

15 Which two old tough guys played a couple of old tough guys in 1986?

16 Which A-list star began his big screen acting career in the low budget 80s slasher movie, *He Knows You're Alone* (1980)?

17 'With great power comes great responsibility. This is my gift, my curse. Who am I?'

18 In which film did poor old Robert Duvall attempt a Scottish accent . . . and fail?

19 What does the 'J' stand for in Michael J. Fox?

20 Who was the only actor who refused to sing in Woody Allen's 1996 musical *Everyone Says I Love You*, insisting, instead, on a voice double?

21 Which actor's real name is Albert Einstein?

22 After which New York City neighbourhood did Robert De Niro name his production company?

23 What was the original title for *Scream* (1996)?

24 In which film would you find a Kit Kat, a Snickers, a Butterfinger and an Almond Joy?

25 In which film did Bruce Willis rescue Julia Roberts from Death Row?

26 What was the name of the 1979 musical supposedly based on the life of the legendary song and dance man, Bob Fosse?

27 The cast and crew of *A Fish Called Wanda* (1988) were reunited nine years later for a sequel that wasn't a sequel. What was the name of that film?

28 In which film did Ferris Bueller reappear in an uncredited cameo?

29 Which *Reservoir Dogs* (1992) character is supposed to be the brother of Vincent Vega (John Travolta) in *Pulp Fiction* (1994)?

30 What was the first all-computer generated animated feature film?

32   DIRECTOR'S CUT

32.1 – THE BACK CATALOGUE

Who directed these films?

1 *Flatliners* (1990)
2 *Cruising* (1980)
3 *The Last Boy Scout* (1991)
4 *Tess* (1979)
5 *Being Human* (1993)
6 *Birdy* (1984)
7 *Ghosts of Mississippi* (1996)
8 *Gallipoli* (1981)
9 *Nuns on the Run* (1990)
10 *Grand Canyon* (1991)
11 *Hulk* (2003)
12 *Flesh & Blood* (1985)
13 *Legend* (1985)
14 *The Portrait of a Lady* (1996)
15 *Swing Shift* (1984)
16 *Agnes of God* (1985)
17 *The People vs. Larry Flynt* (1996)
18 *The Long Kiss Goodnight* (1996)
19 *The Company of Wolves* (1984)
20 *Yanks* (1979)

32.2 – TWO OF A KIND

Two people. One type. Just decide who it was standing behind the camera.

1 SCARY – John Carpenter or Wes Craven: *The Serpent and the Rainbow* (1988)

2 COOL – Steven Soderbergh or Paul Thomas Anderson: *Punch-Drunk Love* (2002)

3 EPIC – Richard Attenborough or David Lean: *A Passage to India* (1984)

4 UNIQUE – Alex Cox or John Waters: *Polyester* (1981)

5 ACTION – John McTiernan or Walter Hill: *Predator* (1987)

6 BOX OFFICE – Steven Spielberg or Ron Howard: *Empire of the Sun* (1987)

7 SOPPY – Nora Ephron or Penny Marshall: *Awakenings* (1990)

8 CULT – David Lynch or Tim Burton: *Lost Highway* (1997)

9 CHILDISH – John Hughes or Chris Columbus: *Curly Sue* (1991)

10 COMICAL – John Landis or Ivan Reitman: *Spies Like Us* (1985)

11 SERIOUS – Sidney Lumet or Alan J. Pakula: *Presumed Innocent* (1990)

12 MASTERS – Francis Ford Coppola or Martin Scorsese: *One from the Heart* (1982)

13 ANGRY – Spike Lee or Oliver Stone: *Talk Radio* (1988)

14 MAVERICK – Robert Altman or Stanley Kubrick: *Full Metal Jacket* (1987)

15 INDEPENDENT – Whit Stillman or Jim Jarmusch: *Barcelona* (1994)

16 GLOSSY – Michael Mann or Adrian Lynne: *Jacob's Ladder* (1990)

17 GLOOMY – Ken Loach or Mike Leigh: *Carla's Song* (1996)

32.3 – THE TRIVIA

1 Which three directors helmed *New York Stories* (1989)?

2 What was the name of the 1987 film directed by John Boorman which chronicled his wartime experiences as a child?

3 Tim Burton's 1994 movie *Ed Wood* recounted the story of the man affectionately dubbed 'the worst director of all time'. Who played the part of the cross-dressing director and what was the name of his now infamous 1959 sci-fi flick?

4 Which 2002 documentary chronicled the disastrous attempts of Terry Gilliam to film his much-cherished project *The Man Who Killed Don Quixote*?

5 Which true-life artist did director Martin Scorsese play in Akira Kurosawa's *Dreams* (1990)?

6 What was the name of the 1990 Clint Eastwood film that supposedly chronicled the film director John Huston's real-life experiences in Africa while shooting *The African Queen* (1951)?

7 Which director is also the voice of Miss Piggy, Fozzie Bear, The Cookie Monster and Yoda?

8 Which famous film director played the part of a famous film director in the third Austin Powers film?

9 The Ismail Merchant–James Ivory director/producer team were responsible for many famous costume dramas during the 1980s and 1990s such as *The Bostonians* (1984), *Howards End* (1992) and *Jefferson in Paris* (1995), but who was the director and who was the producer?

10 In which Steven Spielberg movie did French director François Truffaut appear as a scientist?

And finally . . .

What is the pseudonym traditionally used by directors when they want to disassociate themselves from a bad film?

33.1 – ONLY IN THE MOVIES

Identify which actor had these big-screen family ties?

1   She was Steve Martin's WIFE in *Parenthood* (1989)
2   She was Walter Matthau's NIECE in *IQ* (1994)
3   He was Gene Hackman's SON in *Target* (1985)
4   She was Jack Lemmon's DAUGHTER-IN-LAW in *Missing* (1982)
5   She was Meryl Streep's MOTHER in *Postcards from the Edge* (1990)
6   He was Kurt Russell's BROTHER in *Backdraft* (1991)
7   He was Brad Pitt's FATHER in *Legends of the Fall* (1994)
8   He was Minnie Driver's BOYFRIEND in *Good Will Hunting* (1998)
9   She was Aidan Quinn's SISTER in *Benny & Joon* (1993)
10   She was Joe Pesci's GIRLFRIEND in *My Cousin Vinny* (1992)
11   He was Nicole Kidman's HUSBAND in *My Life* (1993)
12   She was Holly Hunter's DAUGHTER in *The Piano* (1993)
13   She was Gwyneth Paltrow's MOTHER-IN-LAW in *Hush* (1998)
14   He was Marlon Brando's NEPHEW in *The Freshman* (1990)
15   She was William H. Macy's WIFE in *Jurassic Park III* (2001)
16   She was Julia Roberts' SISTER in *Something to Talk About* (1995)
17   He was Goldie Hawn's EX-HUSBAND in *Seems Like Old Times* (1980)
18   He was Mark Wahlberg's UNCLE in *The Yards* (2000)
19   He was Matthew McConaughey's BROTHER in *EdTV* (1999)
20   She was Matt Dillon's EX-WIFE in *Mr Wonderful* (1993)
21   He was Leonardo Di Caprio's GRANDFATHER in *Marvin's Room* (1996)
22   He was Jessica Lange's FATHER in *Music Box* (1989)
23   She was John Candy's MOTHER in *Only the Lonely* (1991)
24   He was Sean Connery's GRANDSON in *Family Business* (1989)
25   She was Ed Harris's EX-WIFE in *Stepmom* (1998)
26   He was Nicolas Cage's BROTHER in *Adaptation* (2002)
27   She was Sigourney Weaver's DAUGHTER in *Heartbreakers* (2001)

28 She was Rob Lowe's GIRLFRIEND in *About Last Night* (1986)
29 She was Kevin Kline's WIFE in *Consenting Adults* (1992)
30 He was Glenne Headley's HUSBAND in *Mortal Thoughts* (1991)

33.2 – REAL LIFE

... And who is really related to whom?

1 He's Julia's brother.
2 She's Michael's granddaughter, Vanessa's daughter, Joely's sister and Liam's wife.
3 The brother of River and Rain, he himself was once a leaf.
4 Named after her father! She is Ethel and Lionel's great-niece, John's granddaughter and Steven's godchild.
5 He's Shirley's brother and Annette's wife.
6 He's John's son, David's brother and Martha's father.
7 He's Kim's husband and the eldest brother of William, Stephen and Daniel.
8 She's Bridget's aunt, Peter's sister and Henry's daughter.
9 He's Leo's son, Chris's brother, Robin's husband and Madonna's ex.
10 He's Carmine's son, Talia's brother, Nic's uncle and Sophia's father.

?₂?   *34   OSCAR*

34.1 – THE FILMS

1   2003   *Chicago* (2002): What was Billy Flynn's fee?

2   2002   *A Beautiful Mind* (2001): Which university did John Nash attend?

3   2001   *Gladiator* (2000): Where did Maximus fight his last battle for the Emperor Marcus Aurelius?

4   2000   *American Beauty* (1999): Who shot Lester?

5   1999   *Shakespeare in Love* (1998): What was the original title of *Romeo and Juliet*?

6   1998   *Titanic* (1997): Who were the owners of the *Titanic*?

7   1997   *The English Patient* (1996): What nationality was 'The English Patient'?

8   1996   *Braveheart* (1995): Which English king was the adversary of William Wallace?

9   1995   *Forrest Gump* (1994): Which ex-Beatle did Forrest meet?

10   1994   *Schindler's List* (1993): What colour was the little girl's coat?

11   1993   *Unforgiven* (1992): Of which town was Little Bill the sheriff?

12   1992   *Silence of the Lambs* (1991): What was the name of the serial killer Clarice wanted Hannibal to help her catch?

13   1991   *Dances with Wolves* (1990): What was the name of the wolf befriended by John Dunbar?

14   1990   *Driving Miss Daisy* (1989): Who hired the chauffeur?

15   1989   *Rain Man* (1988): What was the name of the TV programme that Raymond was so desperate not to miss?

16   1988   *The Last Emperor* (1987): Of where?

17   1987   *Platoon* (1986): Which platoon did Chris Taylor join?

18   1986   *Out of Africa* (1985): Which type of plantation did Karen Blixen-Finecke own with her husband in Kenya?

19   1985   *Amadeus* (1984): Who was of the opinion that Mozart's music had 'simply too many notes'?

20 1984 *Terms of Endearment* (1983): What did Aurora's next-door neighbour do for a living before retiring?

21 1983 *Gandhi* (1982): What was he before becoming India's spiritual leader?

22 1982 *Chariots of Fire* (1981): At which Olympic Games did the British duo of Liddell and Abrahams triumph?

23 1981 *Ordinary People* (1980): How did Conrad's brother die?

24 1980 *Kramer vs. Kramer* (1979): Why did Ted and Joanna Kramer go to court?

25 1979 *The Deer Hunter* (1978): Which 'game' were the American POWs made to play?

34.2 – THE TRIVIA

1 Which film won the first ever BEST ANIMATED PICTURE award in 2002?

2 Only three films have won all of the top five coveted Oscars for Best Picture, Director, Actor, Actress and Screenplay. The first two to achieve this accolade were: *It Happened One Night* (1934) and *One Flew Over the Cuckoo's Nest* (1975). Which was the third?

3 Who was the only person to win an Oscar playing a member of the opposite sex?

4 Who famously refused their Best Actor gong in protest against Hollywood's portrayal of native Americans?

5 Which was the only X-rated film in Oscar's long history to win Best Picture?

6 Who was the first actor to win a Best Actor award for a non-English speaking role?

7 For which two films did Katharine Hepburn and Barbra Streisand share the Best Actress award in 1968?

8 Which only other two westerns before 1992's *Unforgiven* have won Best Picture?

9 Which director holds the record with four wins?

10 Which film won Sean Connery his only Academy Award?

11 Jack Palance holds the record for the longest gap between nomination and victory. After being nominated in 1952 for *Sudden Fear*, he finally achieved Oscar glory forty years later as Best Supporting Actor for which film?

12 Which is the only sequel to win a Best Picture Oscar?

13 What was so notable about Greer Garson's 1943 acceptance speech for her Best Actress Oscar?

14 How was history made at the 2002 ceremony when the Best Actor and Best Actress Oscars were awarded?

15 In which year was the Oscar ceremony first televised?
    (a)   1953
    (b)   1959
    (c)   1961

And finally . . .

Who was the only Oscar winner to play an Oscar loser?

34.3 – THE WINNERS

Who won . . . ?

1 BEST SUPPORTING ACTRESS (2000) for *Girl, Interrupted* (1999)

2 BEST SUPPORTING ACTOR (1999) for *Affliction* (1997)

3 BEST ACTOR (1990) for *My Left Foot* (1989)

4 BEST ACTRESS (1981) for *Coalminer's Daughter* (1980)

5 BEST SUPPORTING ACTRESS (1981) for *Melvin and Howard* (1980)

6 BEST ACTOR (1984) for *Tender Mercies* (1983)
7 BEST ACTRESS (2000) for *Boys Don't Cry* (1999)
8 BEST SUPPORTING ACTOR (2002) for *Iris* (2001)
9 BEST ACTOR (1997) for *Shine* (1996)
10 BEST SUPPORTING ACTRESS (1996) for *Mighty Aphrodite* (1995)
11 BEST SUPPORTING ACTOR (2000) for *The Cider House Rules* (1999)
12 BEST ACTRESS (1985) for *Places in the Heart* (1984)
13 BEST ACTRESS (1980) for *Norma Rae* (1979)
14 BEST ACTOR (1991) for *Reversal of Fortune* (1990)
15 BEST SUPPORTING ACTRESS (1992) for *The Fisher King* (1991)
16 BEST ACTOR (1986) for *Kiss of the Spider Woman* (1985)
17 BEST SUPPORTING ACTRESS (1982) for *Reds* (1981)
18 BEST ACTOR (1979) for *Coming Home* (1978)
19 BEST SUPPORTING ACTOR (1978) for *Julia* (1977)
20 BEST ACTRESS (1986) for *The Trip to Bountiful* (1985)

❓ 35 SPECIFICS

ADVENTURE

1 *The Perfect Storm* (2000): What was the name of the ill-fated fishing boat?

2 *Medicine Man* (1992): What was his nickname for her?

3 *Back to the Future* (1985): At what speed did Marty have to travel in the DeLorean to go back in time?

CHICK FLICKS

4 *Serendipity* (2001): She wrote her phone number on the inside cover of a book. Where did he write his?

5 *It Could Happen to You* (1994): How much was the winning lottery ticket?

6 *You've Got Mail* (1998): What was the name of her shop?

CRIME

7 *L.A. Confidential* (1997): What was the name of the TV show for which Jack Vincennes was a technical advisor?

8 *Pulp Fiction* (1994): 'I do believe Marsellus Wallace, my husband, your boss, told you to take me out ... ' So, where did Vincent take Mia?

9 *The Long Good Friday* (1980): Who was Harold trying to impress?

COMEDY

10 *City Slickers* (1991): What was the cow's name?

11 *Michael* (1996): Where did Michael live?

12 *There's Something About Mary* (1998): What did Mary think was in her hair?

FAMILY

13 *Harry Potter* (2001–05): The Hogwarts Express leaves from which platform at King's Cross station?

14 *Jingle All the Way* (1996): What was the name of that much sought-after toy?

15 *Casper* (1995): What were the names of Casper's three less-than-friendly ghostly pals?

WAR

16 *Black Hawk Down* (2001): 'We got a bird down in the city.' What was the codename of that first downed helicopter and in which city?

17 *We Were Soldiers* (2002): Which famous General had previously commanded the 7th Cavalry?

18 *Victory* (1981): What was the final score in the football match?

HORROR

19 *The Ring* (2003): Having watched the cursed videotape, how long do you have to live?

20 *Candyman* (1992–99): How many times do you need to say his name?

21 *The Thing* (1982): Which country's base camp was first attacked by The Thing?

DRAMA

22 *Glengarry Glenn Ross* (1992): What did Blake's 'ABC' stand for?

23 *Chocolat* (2000): What was Anouk's imaginary friend?

24 *Being John Malkovich* (1999): How much was a fifteen-minute joyride in John Malkovich's mind?

ACTION

25 *The Core* (2003): What was the name of the secret government project that was to be implemented if the mission failed?

26 *Armageddon* (1998): What were the names of the two space shuttles?

27 *True Lies* (1994): What type of jet was Harry Tasker piloting in the film's climax?

THRILLER

28 *The Game* (1997): What was the name of the company that organised The Game?

29 *The Bourne Identity* (2002): How much did Jason Bourne pay Marie to drive him to Paris?

30 *Kalifornia* (1993): Which infamous landmarks were the two couples visiting?

SCIENCE FICTION

31 *Starship Troopers* (1997): Which city did the aliens destroy?

32 *Solaris* (2003): Who was Chris Kelvin's 'visitor'?

33 *Outland* (1981): William T. O'Neil was the Marshall of a remote mining colony on which of Jupiter's four moons?

DOCUMENTARY

34 *When We Were Kings* (1996): What was the 'other name' given to the Ali–Foreman boxing match in Zaire?

35 *Roger & Me* (1989): Who was Roger?

36 *Buena Vista Social Club* (1999): In which famous venue did the band hold their final climactic concert?

BRITISH CINEMA

37 *Birthday Girl* (2001): What was the name of the online dating agency?

38 *The Draughtsman's Contract* (1982): How many portraits of her husband's estate did Mrs Herbert commission?

39 *The Full Monty* (1997): What was their stage name?

HISTORICAL

40 *The Last of the Mohicans* (1992): At which Fort was Colonel Munro stationed?

41 *The Man in the Iron Mask* (1998): Which of the Musketeers remained loyal to the King?

42 *The Mission* (1986): Where did Father Gabriel build his mission?

ANIMATION

43 *Ice Age* (2002): What was the name of the acorn-loving sabre-toothed squirrel?

44 *Fantasia 2000* (2000): Which was the only segment from the original 1940s film to be included with the seven new sequences filmed for this sequel?

45 *Monsters, Inc.* (2001): Where did Mike take Celia Mae on their big date?

COPS

46 *Internal Affairs* (1990): Who was investigating who?

47 *Stakeout* (1987): How did Chris first gain access to Maria's house . . . with her in it?

48 *Alien Nation* (1988): What made the 'Newcomers' drunk?

?¿? 36 TRUE OR FALSE

Be careful. When they're false, they're almost true!

1 *Still Crazy* (1998): The name of the band was 'Soft Fruit'.

2 *Death to Smoochy* (2002): Smoochy was a Hippo.

3 *Untamed Heart* (1993): Adam thought he had the heart of a lion.

4 *The Paper* (1994): The name of the aforementioned tabloid was the *New York Sun*.

5 *Frantic* (1988): Richard Walker was searching for his missing daughter.

6 *Miss Congeniality* (2000): FBI agent Gracie Hart went undercover as Miss Texas in a beauty pageant.

7 *Master and Commander – The Far Side of the World* (2003): 'Lucky' Jack Aubrey was the captain of the HMS *Surprise*.

8 *Spider-Man* (2002): It was the *Daily Bugle* that first gave Peter Parker his nickname of Spider-Man.

9 *Vertical Limit* (2000): Peter Garrett was forced to confront his fear of mountaineering and launch a rescue attempt for his brother who was stranded somewhere on Mount Everest.

10 *Meet Joe Black* (1998): William Parrish was due to die on his 65th birthday.

11 *The Mighty Ducks* (1992–96): The Ducks were a kids' baseball team.

12 *Forget Paris* (1995): Mickey Gordon was a basketball referee who travelled to France to bury his father.

13 *Working Girl* (1988): The wicked Ms Parker broke her leg in a skiing accident.

14 *Broken Arrow* (1996): A military term used for a lost or stolen nuclear weapon.

15 *Mermaids* (1990): Lou Landsky owned a grocer's shop.

16 *If Lucy Fell* (1996): Lucy and Joe decided to throw themselves off the Golden Gate Bridge if they didn't find true love in thirty days.

17 *Short Circuit* (1986): It was Robot #4 that escaped from the factory.

18 *Coming to America* (1988): Prince Akeem of Zamunda got himself a job as a cleaner in McDowell's Burger Bar.

19 *Manhattan Murder Mystery* (1993): Carol Lipton suspected her husband of murdering the woman next door.

20 *Cocoon* (1985): The old folks were rejuvenated by swimming in a pool containing the alien pods.

21 *The Warriors* (1979): After being wrongly accused of killing a rival gang leader, the Warriors tried to reach their 'home turf' of Coney Island.

22 *The Right Stuff* (1983): The epic story of America's Jupiter space program.

23 *Breaking Away* (1979): Dave was obsessed with all things French.

24 *Enemy at the Gates* (2001): A Russian and German sniper played a game of cat-and-mouse with each other during World War II's Battle of Stalingrad.

25 *Thelma & Louise* (1991): Louise refused to drive through Kentucky enroute to Mexico.

26 *Patch Adams* (1998): Hunter 'Patch' Adams was famous for wearing a big red nose to help make sick kids laugh.

27 *The Ninth Gate* (1999): Dean Corso was seeking the last two remaining copies of a book called *The Ninth Gate of the Kingdom of Shadows*.

28 *Almost Famous* (2000): William's exposé of rock band Stillwater made the front cover of *Time* magazine.

29 *xXx* (2002): The bad guys called themselves 'Anarchy 99'.

30 *Where the Heart Is* (2000): Novalee had her baby in a Wal-Mart store.

? *37* **BEHIND THE SCENES**

This one may be a little difficult . . . even with the answers!

37.1 – THE WRITERS

Who wrote the screenplay for these films?

1 *Greedy* (1994)
2 *The Last Boy Scout* (1991)
3 *Jade* (1995)
4 *State and Main* (2000)
5 *Memories of Me* (1988)

ANSWERS: Shane Black, Eric Roth, Joe Esterhaus, Lowell Ganz and Babaloo Mandel, David Mamet

37.2 – THE PRODUCERS

Who produced these films?

1 *Jumpin' Jack Flash* (1986)
2 *Remember the Titans* (2000)
3 *Mulholland Falls* (1996)
4 *Wonder Boys* (2000)
5 *The Unbearable Lightness of Being* (1988)

ANSWERS: Lili Fini Zanuck and Richard D. Zanuck, Saul Zaentz, Joel Silver, Jerry Bruckheimer, Scott Rudin

37.3 – THE MUSICIANS

Who composed the music for these films?

1 *Hook* (1991)
2 *Smilla's Sense of Snow* (1997)
3 *The Truth About Cats & Dogs* (1996)
4 *How to Make an American Quilt* (1995)
5 *Powder* (1995)

ANSWERS: John Williams, Hans Zimmer, Howard Shore, Jerry Goldsmith, Thomas Newman

37.4 – THE TECHNICAL SUPPORT

What do these guys do on a film set?

1 The Gaffer
2 The Best Boy
3 The Foley Artist
4 The Greensmen
5 The Swing Gang

37.5 – THE BIZ

1 At what speed (in frames per second) does a 35mm film run through a camera and projector?
2 What does the MGM motto *Ars Gratia Artis* actually mean?
3 In Variety speak, what is a Horse Opera?
4 What is the aspect ratio of a 70mm frame of film?
5 How is the IMAX name derived?

6 Who founded the DreamWorks studio in 1994?
7 Who were Jack, Harry, Albert and Sam?
8 Who currently owns the 'Lady with the Torch'?
9 What does the abbreviation 'EXT' mean in a screenplay?
10 What do the initials MPAA stand for?

38 THE END REEL ?

1 Who played the pest exterminator in *Mouse Hunt* (1997)?

2 What was the name of the big fat man who exploded after eating too much in *Monty Python's The Meaning of Life* (1983)?

3 *T.J. Hooker – The Movie* exists only as a film-within-a-film in which movie?

4 Which 1988 John Sayles drama chronicled the true story of the underpaid Chicago White Sox baseball team which accepted bribes to deliberately lose the 1919 World Series?

5 What was the nickname given to the K19 submarine by its crew?

6 Who went on the run with William Baldwin in *Fair Game* (1995)?

7 Which cop went undercover in a kindergarten?

8 #3 was a sequel to #2, but #2 was no more than a big-bucks remake of #1. What was #3's south-of-the-border fairytale title?

9 Who was looking for *The Sure Thing* in California?

10 Which 1983 film starred David Bowie as a vampire?

11 In which 1988 comedy-thriller did Rebecca De Mornay train to be an FBI agent?

12 What was *Bendini, Lambert and Locke* better known as?

13 What was the name of the actress played by Kim Basinger in *L.A. Confidential* (1997)?

14 ... And the one played by Annette Bening in *Bugsy* (1981)?

15 Who was competing against Steve Martin for that seemingly unobtainable 'cab-for-hire' at the beginning of *Planes, Trains and Automobiles* (1987)?

16 In 1983 the four old grandmasters of horror; Vincent Price, Christopher Lee, Peter Cushing and John Carradine shared the big screen together for the first time. Something about spooky goings-on in a haunted house. What was the name of that film?

17 Where were *The Killing Fields* (1984)?

18 What was the name of the spaceship that carried the Robinson family into space?

19 How many people were trapped in the *Cube* (1997)?

20 What was the name of Patsy Kensit's character in the 1986 flop musical *Absolute Beginners*?

21 In which film did the US government attempt to fake a manned space flight to Mars?

22 *The Outsiders* (1983) was one of two S.E. Hinton novels about rebellious youth filmed back-to-back by Francis Ford Coppola in the early 1980s. What was the title of the other film?

23 What do you call a throw of two dice that turns up one spot on each?

24 Which of Pooh's friends got his own movie in 2003?

25 In which film did Michael Keaton play a snowman?

26 Who captained the HMS *Bounty* in 1984?

27 Who was the money-grabbing bitch that married poor old Uncle Fester just for his money?

28 Where did Pluto Nash own a nightclub?

29 What was the name of the Philip K. Dick short story that inspired *Total Recall* (1990)?

30 The *Lucky Break* (2001) prison inmates staged a musical show about which famous British historical figure in order to distract the guards and make their escape?

31 What was the last animated Disney film to be drawn entirely by hand?

32 Which loveable screen mutt took his name from a famous composer?

33 Who or what is Zion?

34 Which 2003 movie was inspired by a popular Walt Disney theme park ride of the same name?

35 Which 1999 prison drama's timeframe was moved forward three years from the book's original 1932 setting, so a scene featuring the movie *Top Hat* (1935) could be included?

36 What is a *D.A.R.Y.L.* (1985)?

37 In which film did Donald Sutherland play a Nazi spy who discovered the secrets of the D-Day landings?

38 What was Casey Ryback's job aboard the USS *Missouri*?
39 Which country's dead President did the little known American actor Jack Noah impersonate after his sudden death?
40 In which film did the American poetess Joy Grisham embark on a tragic love affair with the famous author C.S. Lewis?

??? 39 TOO DIFFICULT

Like, all the rest were easy!

1 What was the name of the fictitious lost tribe of New Guinea 'discovered' by James Krippendorf?
2 What's the phone number of Morrie's Wig shop?
3 Who directed the kitschy horror film *Mant!* (1962)?
4 Which Bruce Springsteen song inspired Sean Penn to write *The Indian Runner* (1991)?
5 In *Clueless* speak, who or what is a 'Baldwin'?
6 What was on the corner of 8th Avenue and 53rd Street?
7 Esther, Ruth and who else?
8 Why was Andrew Clark in detention?
9 Just how many lovers did Carrie have (including Charles and her fiancé)?
10 Who worked at the Kerr McGee nuclear power plant?
11 *See You Next Wednesday* is the title of an imaginary movie often featured in which director's films?
12 What were Ned's winning lottery numbers ... oh, and how much did he win?
13 Who appeared in 63 episodes of the popular daytime soap opera *A Reason to Love*?
14 What was discovered on the island of Cascara?
15 Cirrus. Socrates. Particle. Decibel, Hurricane. Dolphin ...

40   THE FINAL QUESTION ?

The answer to the final question should be rather obvious.

1 The title of a 1978 black comedy in which a man tries to commit
  suicide on learning that he only has six months to live.

ANSWERS

1 TOO EASY

1. Videotape/*Sex, Lies and Videotape* (1989) **2.** 4 Weddings and 1 Funeral/ *Four Weddings and a Funeral* (1994) **3.** Harrison Ford **4.** Steven Spielberg **5.** A Hobbit/*Lord of the Rings* (2001–03) **6.** Hooch/*Turner & Hooch* (1989) **7.** Michael Jordan/*Space Jam* (1996) **8.** R2-D2 and C-3PO **9.** 3/*Back to the Future* (1985–90) **10.** The Godfather/*The Godfather Part III* (1990) **11.** Danny DeVito **12.** Captain Jean-Luc Picard/Patrick Stewart in *Star Trek* (1994–2002) **13.** *Die Hard* (1988–2004) **14.** Kevin McCallister/Macaulay Culkin in *Home Alone* (1990) **15.** A mouse/*Stuart Little* (1999–2002).

2 THE NAME GAME

1. Billy Crystal **2.** Keanu Reeves **3.** Diane Keaton **4.** Sam Rockwell and Joe Mantegna **5.** Clint Eastwood **6.** Michael J. Fox **7.** Kurt Russell **8.** Kathleen Turner **9.** Jodie Foster **10.** Denzel Washington **11.** Kim Basinger **12.** Adam Sandler **13.** John Turturro **14.** Robert De Niro and Uma Thurman **15.** Steve McQueen **16.** Jim Carrey, Jim Carrey and Renée Zellweger **17.** Vanessa Redgrave **18.** Robin Williams **19.** Kathy Bates **20.** Demi Moore **21.** Michelle Pfeiffer and Al Pacino **22.** Johnny Depp **23.** Julia Roberts **24.** Richard Gere **25.** Ralph Fiennes and Cate Blanchett **26.** Lolita Davidovich **27.** Liam Neeson **28.** Salma Hayek **29.** Paul Newman and Joanne Woodward **30.** Mia Farrow, Barbara Hershey and Dianne Wiest.

3 WHODUNNIT

1. Wesley Snipes **2.** Goldie Hawn **3.** Kevin Costner **4.** Robert De Niro **5.** Michael Keaton **6.** Robin Wright Penn **7.** Meg Ryan **8.** Danny DeVito **9.** Jean-Claude Van Damme **10.** Russell Crowe **11.** Jodie Foster **12.** Michelle Pfeiffer **13.** Clint Eastwood **14.** Michael J. Fox and/or James Woods **15.** Steven Seagal **16.** Cate Blanchett **17.** Jeff Goldblum and/or Michelle Pfeiffer **18.** Nick Nolte **19.** Gérard Depardieu **20.** Ewan McGregor

21. Tom Selleck **22.** Tom Hanks **23.** Morgan Freeman **24.** Diane Lane **25.** Drew Barrymore **26.** Jackie Chan **27.** Nicolas Cage **28.** Gene Hackman **29.** Will Smith **30.** Campbell Scott.

4 SAME OLD, SAME OLD

4.1 SUBTITLES

1. *Sister Act 2 – Back in the Habit* (1993) **2.** *City Slickers II – The Legend of Curly's Gold* (1994) **3.** *Superman IV – The Quest for Peace* (1987) **4.** *Arthur 2 – On the Rocks* (1988) **5.** *Terminator 3 – Rise of the Machines* (2003) **6.** *Home Alone 2 – Lost in New York* (1992) **7.** *Airplane II – The Sequel* (1982) **8.** *Gremlins 2 – The New Batch* (1990) **9.** *Highlander II – The Quickening* (1991) **10.** *Homeward Bound II – Lost in San Francisco* (1996) **11.** *White Fang II – Myth of the White Wolf* (1994) **12.** *F/X 2 – The Deadly Art of Illusion* (1991) **13.** *Hellraiser III – Hell on Earth* (1992) **14.** *Legally Blonde 2 – Red, White and Blonde* (2003) **15.** *Spy Kids 2 – Island of Lost Dreams* (2002).

4.2 SOMETHING DIFFERENT

1. *I Know What You Did Last Summer* (1997) **2.** *The Fast and the Furious* (2001) **3.** *Honey, I Shrunk the Kids* (1989) **4.** *The Brady Bunch Movie* (1995) **5.** *The Whole Nine Yards* (2000) **6.** *Beyond the Poseidon Adventure* (1979) **7.** *Force 10 from Navarone* (1978) **8.** *More American Graffiti* (1979) **9.** *Return from the River Kwai* (1988) **10.** *Return to Oz* (1985) **11.** *Chinatown* (1974) **12.** *The Last Picture Show* (1971) **13.** *Saturday Night Fever* (1977) **14.** *Terms of Endearment* (1983) **15.** *Love Story* (1970).

4.3 THE NUMBERS

1. 3 (1987–93) **2.** 5 (1976–90) **3.** 7 (1984–94) **4.** 4 – including *The Next Karate Kid* (1994) (1984–94) **5.** 8 (1978–2002) **6.** 7 (1984–2001) **7.** 2 (1991–94) **8.** 6 (1979–99) – *The Muppet Movie* (1979), *The Great Muppet*

Caper (1981), *The Muppets Take Manhattan* (1984), *The Muppet Christmas Carol* (1992), *Muppet Treasure Island* (1996), *Muppets from Space* (1999) **9.** 4 (1979–97) **10.** 3 (1982–88) **11.** 4 (1975–87) **12.** 3 (1979–85) **13.** 4 (1986–95) **14.** 3 (1998–2003) **15.** 4 (2000–04).

4.4 FIRST THINGS FIRST

1. *Bill & Ted's Excellent Adventure* (1989)/(1991) **2.** *Every Which Way But Loose* (1978)/(1980) **3.** *Analyze This* (1999)/(2002) **4.** *Escape from New York* (1981)/(1996) **5.** *Conan the Barbarian* (1982)/(1984) **6.** *Three Men and a Baby* (1987)/(1990) **7.** *Look Who's Talking Too* (1990)/(1993) **8.** *Matrix Reloaded* (2003)/(2003) **9.** *An American Werewolf in London* (1981)/(1997) **10.** *Shanghai Noon* (2000)/(2003).

4.5 THE IMPOSTER

1. (c) **2.** (b) **3.** (a) – *A Nightmare on Elm Street Part 2 – Freddy's Revenge* **4.** (d) **5.** (b).

4.6 THE TRIVIA

1. There never was a 'Part 2' **2.** *Freddy vs. Jason* (2003) **3.** Annie Porter (Sandra Bullock)/*Speed* (1994) and *Speed 2 – Cruise Control* (1997) **4.** The Two Towers/Lord of the Rings – *The Two Towers* (2002) **5.** Roberto Benigni **6.** Queen Elizabeth II/*The Naked Gun* (1988) **7.** England/*National Lampoon's European Vacation* (1985) **8.** Wesley Snipes/*U.S. Marshals* (1998) **9.** Adolf Hitler/*Indiana Jones and the Last Crusade* (1989) **10.** Vigo The Carpathian **11.** Wonder World **12.** #2/*Lethal Weapon 2* (1989) **13.** Site B/*The Lost World: Jurassic Park* (1997) and *Jurassic Park III* (2001) **14.** *Naqoyqatsi* (2002) **15.** *American Wedding* (2003) **And finally . . .** 'A sequel'.

5 FIFTY FIFTY

1. Sex – After a bust-up with his girlfriend, Matt vowed to stay celibate for the forty days of Lent. **2. Starbucks** – The shop where Sam worked. **3. Cookies** – Ray and Frenchy owned a cookie shop, as a 'front' for their other illegal activities. **4. Rita Hayworth** – The poster on Andy's cell wall at the start of his prison sentence was a pin-up of Rita Hayworth. **5. M.I.T.** – The college where Will worked as a janitor. **6. Ex-Presidents** – The disguises used by the bank robbers were face mask caricatures of former US Presidents. **7. Train** – Helen's life changed forever when she missed catching an underground train. **8. Filofax** – Spencer's life was turned upside down when he lost his Filofax. **9. Elvis Presley** – Clarence's mentor was Elvis Presley. **10. Alabama** – Billy was on trial for murder in Alabama. **11. Gold** – A small group of soldiers set out to steal a huge cache of gold hidden somewhere in the Kuwait desert. **12. Scrabble** – Mary liked to play Scrabble with her father. **13. Navajo** – The language used as a basis for a secret wartime code. **14. Whales** – Saving the whales in the twentieth century was the key to saving the world in the twenty-third century. **15. Bus** – Joe drove a bus full of kids across country. **16. Spiders** – Mechanical spiders were used to search the building in which John Anderton was hiding. **17. 21** – The name of the game show on which Charles Van Dorren appeared as a contestant. **18. Cigarettes** – Lowell Bergman investigated malpractice in the tobacco industry. **19. Rugby** – It was the Uruguayan rugby team's plane that crashed in the Andes. **20. Pigs** – It was a stolen pig that was to be the centrepiece of a celebratory dinner. **21. Nike** – The advertising campaign was for Nike. **22. Cards** – Mike and Lester were poker players. **23. Quantas** – The only airline that Raymond would fly. **24. Democrat** – The Senator's political persuasion. **25. Monet** – The stolen painting. **26. Thanksgiving** – Neal Page was travelling from New York to Chicago to spend Thanksgiving with his family. **27. Clint Eastwood** – The false name used by Marty McFly. **28. Chess** – The film's sporty background. **29. Japan** – Where Jack Elliott played out his last days as a professional baseball star. **30. Tango** – Frank Slade danced the Tango on his weekend visit to New York.

6 LINKS

6.1 THE COMMON ONE

1. THINGS/*Needful Things* (1993) and *Very Bad Things* (1998)
2. PEOPLE/*Ordinary People* (1980) and *Ruthless People* (1986) **3.** BOYS/
Boys on the Side (1995) and *The Boys Next Door* (1986) **4.** DANCE/*Dance
with a Stranger* (1985) and *Dance with Me* (1998) **5.** SPACE/*Space
Cowboys* (2000) and *Space Truckers* (1997) **6.** BLUE/*Blue Velvet* (1986)
and *Blue Steel* (1990) **7.** RAIN/*Hard Rain* (1998) and *Black Rain* (1989)
8. MEASURES/*Desperate Measures* (1998) and *Extreme Measures* (1996)
9. FIRE/*Fire in the Sky* (1993) and *Fire Down Below* (1997) **10.** SWEET/
Sweet Dreams (1985) and *Sweet Liberty* (1986).

6.2 THE MISSING ONE

1. WILD/*Something Wild* (1986) and *Wild at Heart* (1990) **2.** YOUNG/*Forever
Young* (1992) and *Young Doctors in Love* (1982) **3.** OUT/*Blow Out* (1981)
and *Out for Justice* (1991) **4.** MONEY/*Milk Money* (1994) and *Money Train*
(1995) **5.** HOME/*Fly Away Home* (1996) and *Home for the Holidays* (1995)
6. AMERICAN/*Everybody's All-American* (1988) and *American Heart* (1992)
7. COMPANY/*Bad Company* (2002) and *Company Business* (1991)
8. CLUB/*The Emperor's Club* (2002) and *Club Paradise* (1986) **9.** HOLLOW/
Sleepy Hollow (1999) and *Hollow Man* (2000) **10.** SLEEPING/*While You Were
Sleeping* (1995) and *Sleeping with the Enemy* (1991).

7 TAGLINES

1. *Men in Black* (1997) **2.** *The Usual Suspects* (1995) **3.** *Vanilla Sky* (2001)
4. *Goodfellas* (1990) **5.** *L.A. Confidential* (1997) **6.** *Mars Attacks!* (1996)
7. *Bulletproof Monk* (2003) **8.** *Scream 2* (1997) **9.** *A Nightmare on Elm
Street* (1984) **10.** *Gosford Park* (2001) **11.** *Deep Impact* (1998) **12.** *A.I. –
Artificial Intelligence* (2001) **13.** *Rush Hour* (1998) **14.** *Interview with the*

Vampire – The Vampire Chronicles (1994) **15.** Panic Room (2002) **16.** The Blair Witch Project (1999) **17.** Robocop (1987) **18.** Bride of Chucky (1998) **19.** Phone Booth (2002) **20.** Scarface (1983) **21.** True Romance (1993) **22.** Series 7 – The Contenders (2001) **23.** Chicago (2002) **24.** The Thing (1982) **25.** Eight Legged Freaks (2002) **26.** Summer of Sam (1999) **27.** The Rock (1996) **28.** The Color of Money (1986) **29.** Serial Mom (1994) **30.** Other People's Money (1991) **31.** The Fly (1986) **32.** Scooby Doo (2002) **33.** Pale Rider (1985) **34.** Wayne's World (1992) **35.** The Truman Show (1999) **36.** About Schmidt (2002) **37.** Scanners (1981) **38.** The Lost Boys (1987) **39.** Predator 2 (1990) **40.** Bringing Out the Dead (1999).

8 SMART TALK

1. The Sixth Sense (1999) **2.** Splash (1984) **3.** Raiders of the Lost Ark (1981) **4.** Jackie Brown (1997) **5.** The Deer Hunter (1978) **6.** Groundhog Day (1993) **7.** Body Heat (1981) **8.** Billy Elliot (2000) **9.** Life of Brian (1979) **10.** Raging Bull (1980) **11.** Pale Rider (1985) **12.** Aliens (1986) **13.** High Fidelity (2000) **14.** Robin Hood – Prince of Thieves (1991) **15.** Toy Story (1995) **16.** Basic Instinct (1992) **17.** Road to Perdition (2002) **18.** When Harry Met Sally . . . (1989) **19.** Manhattan Murder Mystery (1993) **20.** National Lampoon's Christmas Vacation (1989) **21.** Reservoir Dogs (1992) **22.** Beetlejuice (1988) **23.** Twilight Zone – The Movie (1983) **24.** Jerry Maguire (1996) **25.** Apocalypse Now (1979) **26.** The Fabulous Baker Boys (1989) **27.** Ghostbusters (1984) **28.** City Slickers (1991) **29.** Working Girl (1988) **30.** Saving Private Ryan (1998) **31.** Bad Boys (1995) **32.** About a Boy (2002) **33.** Zelig (1983) **34.** Wall Street (1987) **35.** Erin Brockovich (2000) **36.** Two Weeks Notice (2003) **37.** Lethal Weapon (1987) **38.** Tea with Mussolini (1999) **39.** The Untouchables (1987) **40.** The Talented Mr Ripley (2000) **41.** An Officer and a Gentleman (1982) **42.** Braveheart (1995) **43.** Dead Poets Society (1989) **44.** Independence Day (1996) **45.** The Cable Guy (1996).

9 THE CASTING COUCH

9.1 TO DIE FOR

1. *America's Sweethearts* (2001) **2.** *Dangerous Liaisons* (1988) **3.** *Wrestling Ernest Hemingway* (1993) **4.** *Flatliners* (1990) **5.** *The Royal Tenenbaums* (2001) **6.** *The Big Lebowski* (1998) **7.** *Bandits* (2001) **8.** *JFK* (1991) **9.** *The Score* (2001) **10.** *Outbreak* (1995) **11.** *Grand Canyon* (1991) **12.** *U-Turn* (1997) **13.** *Runaway Train* (1985) **14.** *California Suite* (1978) **15.** *Steel Magnolias* (1989) **16.** *Singles* (1992) **17.** *Stealing Beauty* (1996) **18.** *The Natural* (1984) **19.** *Prizzi's Honor* (1985) **20.** *Cold Mountain* (2003) **21.** *The Man in the Iron Mask* (1998) **22.** *Dead Calm* (1989) **23.** *Maid in Manhattan* (2002) **24.** *Bad Girls* (1994) **25.** *The Thin Red Line* (1998).

9.2 ONE TIME ONLY

1. *A Perfect World* (1993) **2.** *Runaway Jury* (2003) **3.** *Heat* (1995) **4.** *The Russia House* (1990) **5.** *Conspiracy Theory* (1997) **6.** *A Few Good Men* (1992) **7.** *The Jackal* (1997) **8.** *Philadelphia* (1993) **9.** *The Devil's Own* (1997) **10.** *The Formula* (1980).

9.3 DEJA VU

1. Aidan Quinn and Madeleine Stowe **2.** Matt Damon and Ben Affleck **3.** Richard Pryor and Gene Wilder **4.** Sam Shepard and Jessica Lange **5.** Nick Nolte and Debra Winger **6.** Richard Gere and Kim Basinger **7.** Anthony Hopkins and Emma Thompson **8.** Dennis Quaid and Meg Ryan **9.** Robert De Niro and Meryl Streep **10.** Steve Martin and Rick Moranis.

9.4 AGAINST TYPE

1. *The Spanish Prisoner* (1997) **2.** *Training Day* (2001) **3.** *One Hour Photo* (2002) **4.** *The Watcher* (2000) **5.** *Casualties of War* (1989) **6.** *Escape to Athena* (1979) **7.** *Grey Owl* (1999) **8.** *The Betsy* (1978) **9.** *Deceived* (1991) **10.** *Ghost Story* (1981).

9.5 SMALL BEGINNINGS

1. BRUCE WILLIS/David Addison in the TV series *Moonlighting* (1985–89) **2.** SHARON STONE/That infamous scene in *Basic Instinct* (1992) in which Ms Stone uncrossed her legs only for the whole world to see that she wasn't wearing any underwear. **3.** KEVIN COSTNER/Alex, the dead friend for whose funeral everyone was reunited. All the scenes featuring Kevin Costner were later deleted from the movie's final cut. Trick question! **4.** CUBA GOODING JR /His famous catchphrase of 'Show me the money!' from *Jerry Maguire* (1996) **5.** JENNIFER GARNER/No relation to James Garner.

10 10 × 10

10.1 MR PRESIDENT

1. Harrison Ford **2.** Michael Douglas **3.** Morgan Freeman **4.** Jack Nicholson **5.** Kevin Kline **6.** Bill Pullman **7.** Anthony Hopkins **8.** Jon Voight **9.** Roy Scheider **10.** Gene Hackman.

10.2 DON'T THEY MAKE A LOVELY COUPLE

1. Patricia Arquette and Christian Slater in *True Romance* (1993) **2.** Jessica Lange and Jack Nicholson in *The Postman Always Rings Twice* (1981) **3.** Jennifer Lopez and George Clooney in *Out of Sight* (1998) **4.** Amanda Plummer and Tim Roth in *Pulp Fiction* (1994) **5.** Juliette Lewis and Woody Harrelson in *Natural Born Killers* (1994) **6.** Katharine Hepburn and Henry Fonda in *On Golden Pond* (1981) **7.** Bette Midler and James Caan in *For the Boys* (1991) **8.** Laura Dern and Nicolas Cage in *Wild at Heart* (1990) **9.** Demi Moore and Patrick Swayze in *Ghost* (1990) **10.** Jennifer Grey and Patrick Swayze in *Dirty Dancing* (1987).

10.3 VILLAINS

1. Gary Oldman **2.** Donald Sutherland **3.** John Malkovich **4.** Tim Robbins **5.** Rebecca De Mornay **6.** John Lithgow **7.** J.T. Walsh **8.** Ray Liotta **9.** Michael Keaton **10.** Nicolas Cage.

10.4 TOUGH GUYS

1. Arnie **2.** Sly **3.** Arnie **4.** Jean-Claude **5.** Arnie **6.** Jean-Claude **7.** Jean-Claude **8.** Sly **9.** Sly **10.** Arnie.

10.5 NOM DE PLUME

1. Men in Black/*Men in Black* (1997–2002) **2.** Santa Claus/*Miracle on 34th Street* (1993) **3.** The Witches of Eastwick/*The Witches of Eastwick* (1987) **4.** Three Amigos/*Three Amigos* (1986) **5.** Superman and Supergirl/*Superman* (1978–87), *Supergirl* (1984) **6.** Spinal Tap/*This Is Spinal Tap* (1984) **7.** The Powerpuff Girls/*The Powerpuff Girls* (2002) **8.** Stitch/*Lilo & Stitch* (2002) **9.** Zorro/*The Mask of Zorro* (1998) **10.** The Untouchables/*The Untouchables* (1987).

10.6 FRIEND OR FOE

1. FOE: Richard Dreyfuss and Danny DeVito in *Tin Men* (1987) **2.** FOE: Ben Affleck and Samuel L. Jackson in *Changing Lanes* (2002) **3.** FOE: Roy Scheider and Jurgen Prochnow in *The Fourth War* (1990) **4.** FRIEND: Jack Lemmon and Walter Matthau in *The Odd Couple* (1968–98) **5.** FOE: Leonardo Di Caprio and Daniel Day Lewis in *Gangs of New York* (2002) **6.** FRIEND: Mira Sorvino and Lisa Kudrow in *Romy and Michele's High School Reunion* (1997) **7.** FOE: Michael Caine and Steve Martin in *Dirty Rotten Scoundrels* (1988) **8.** FOE: Robert De Niro and Charles Grodin in *Midnight Run* (1988) **9.** FOE: Kathleen Turner and Michael Douglas in *The War of the Roses* (1989) **10.** FRIEND: Mickey Rourke and Don Johnson in *Harley Davidson and the Marlboro Man* (1991).

10.7 CREDIT WHERE CREDIT'S DUE

1. Sean Connery **2.** Alec Baldwin **3.** Chazz Palminteri **4.** Danny Glover **5.** Billy Crystal **6.** Whoopi Goldberg **7.** Jeff Bridges **8.** Christopher Lambert **9.** Tom Cruise **10.** Mel Gibson.

10.8 NICKNAMES

1. Madonna in *A League of Their Own* (1992) **2.** John Malkovich in *Con Air* (1997) **3.** Burt Lancaster in *Field of Dreams* (1989) **4.** Charlie Sheen in *Major League* (1989–94) **5.** William H. Macy in *Magnolia* (1999) **6.** Johnny Depp in *Cry-Baby* (1990) **7.** Nicolas Cage in *Gone in 60 Seconds* (2000) **8.** Robert De Niro in *Casino* (1995) **9.** Meg Ryan and Tom Hanks in *You've Got Mail* (1998) **10.** Michael Douglas in *Falling Down* (1993).

10.9 THE SUPPORT

1. Joe Pesci in *Lethal Weapon 2–4* (1989–98) **2.** Heather Graham in *Austin Powers – The Spy Who Shagged Me* (1999) **3.** Rupert Everett in *My Best Friend's Wedding* (1997) **4.** Jack Nicholson in *Terms of Endearment* (1983) **5.** Cameron Diaz in *The Mask* (1994) **6.** Whoopi Goldberg in *Ghost* (1990) **7.** John Turturro in *The Big Lebowski* (1998) **8.** Brad Pitt in *Kalifornia* (1993) **9.** Richard Harris in *Unforgiven* (1992) **10.** Halle Berry in *The Flintstones* (1994).

10.10 FAMOUS NAMES

1. Robert Downey Jr **2.** Angela Bassett **3.** Will Smith **4.** Faye Dunaway **5.** Forrest Whitaker **6.** Dennis Quaid **7.** Ian McKellen **8.** Gary Oldman **9.** Milla Jovovich **10.** Wes Studi.

11 BODY PARTS

1. *Fort Apache, **The Bronx*** (1981) **2.** *Life or Something **Like It*** (2003) **3.** *Chicago Joe and **the Showgirl*** (1990) **4.** *Eternal Sunshine **of the***

Spotless Mind (2003) **5.** *Along Came a Spider* (2001) **6.** *All the Pretty Horses* (2000) **7.** *And Justice For All* (1979) **8.** *My Big Fat Greek Wedding* (2002) **9.** *South Park: Bigger, Longer & Uncut* (1999) **10.** *Things You Can Only Tell Just by Looking at Her* (2000) **11.** *Jo Jo Dancer, Your Life Is Calling* (1986) **12.** *What Dreams May Come* (1998) **13.** *At Play in the Fields of the Lord* (1991) **14.** *Bodies, Rest & Motion* (1993) **15.** *Gas Food Lodging* (1992) **16.** *Midnight in The Garden of Good and Evil* (1997) **17.** *To Wong Foo, Thanks for Everything, Julie Newmar* (1995) **18.** *Merry Christmas, Mr Lawrence* (1982) **19.** *Divine Secrets of the Ya-Ya Sisterhood* (2002) **20.** *Even Cowgirls Get the Blues* (1993) **21.** *Where the Day Takes You* (1992) **22.** *My Own Private Idaho* (1991) **23.** *Come Back to the 5 and Dime Jimmy Dean, Jimmy Dean* (1982) **24.** *Sweet Home Alabama* (2002) **25.** *In Praise of Older Women* (1978) **26.** *Five Days One Summer* (1982) **27.** *So I Married an Axe Murderer* (1993) **28.** *How Stella Got Her Groove Back* (1998) **29.** *Snow Falling on Cedars* (1999) **30.** *Last Exit to Brooklyn* (1989) **31.** *When the Whales Came* (1989) **32.** *Things to Do in Denver When You're Dead* (1995) **33.** *Don't Tell Mom the Babysitter's Dead* (1991) **34.** *Children of a Lesser God* (1986) **35.** *Something Wicked This Way Comes* (1983) **36.** *Full Moon in Blue Water* (1988) **37.** *To Live and Die in L.A.* (1985) **38.** *Stop! Or My Mom Will Shoot* (1992) **39.** *Fear and Loathing in Las Vegas* (1998) **40.** *Twin Peaks: Fire Walk with Me* (1992).

12 WHAT WAS WHAT

1. Aeroplane **2.** Antique pistol **3.** Spaceship **4.** Helicopter **5.** Car (1958 Plymouth Fury) **6.** Planet **7.** Atomic Bombs **8.** Horse **9.** House **10.** Bar **11.** Board Game **12.** TV show **13.** Prison **14.** Computer Security Program **15.** Nightclub **16.** Town **17.** Secret society **18.** Film **19.** Ship **20.** Company **21.** School **22.** Diner **23.** Lions **24.** Play **25.** US Army Regiment **26.** Person **27.** Drug **28.** Team of Cops **29.** Song **30.** Neighbourhood **And Finally . . .** A vast computer-generated illusion created to fool the human race into thinking that they were living in a real world when actually they were being farmed by evil robots . . . or something like that!

13 SHORT AND SWEET

1. Death/*Death Becomes Her* (1992) **2.** The right thing/*Do the Right Thing* (1989) **3.** *Beaches* (1988) **4.** *Child's Play* (1988–98) **5.** *Pi* (1998) **6.** The Bellboy/*Blame It on the Bellboy* (1992) **7.** *Groundhog Day* (1993) **8.** *Charlie's Angels* (2000–03)/Words from the original TV show's voice-over. **9.** *The Opposite of Sex* (1998) **10.** The Game/*For Love of the Game* (1999) **11.** *A Room with a View* (1985) **12.** Texas/*Paris, Texas* (1984) **13.** *Ghostbusters* (1984–89), 555 2368 **14.** In her handbag/*The Gun in Betty Lou's Handbag* (1992) **15.** *Prêt-à-Porter* (1994) **16.** Dance/*Tough Guys Don't Dance* (1987) **17.** 37/*To Gillian on Her 37th Birthday* (1996) **18.** *True Lies* (1994) **19.** *No Way Out* (1987) **20.** *The Morning After* (1986) **21.** A month/*A Month by the Lake* (1995), *A Month in the Country* (1987) **22.** **Batteries Not Included* (1987) **23.** Jump/*White Men Can't Jump* (1992) **24.** *A Zed & Two Noughts* (1985) **25.** She got married/*Peggy Sue Got Married* (1986) **26.** 1954/*My Favorite Year* (1982) **27.** *Almost an Angel* (1990) **28.** *9 to 5* (1980) **29.** *Footloose* (1984) **30.** A fool/*Bert Rigby, You're a Fool* (1989) **31.** A genius/*Jimmy Neutron, Boy Genius* (2001) **32.** Blue/*Mickey Blue Eyes* (1999), *Devil in a Blue Dress* (1995) **33.** *Trainspotting* (1996) **34.** *Insomnia* (2002) **35.** *Monster's Ball* (2001)/Mike and Sully being characters from *Monsters, Inc.* (2001) **36.** Happy/*Happy, Texas* (1999) **37.** *Moulin Rouge* (2001) **38.** *Traffic* (2000) **39.** *Pearl Harbor* (2001)/The date of the Japanese attack. **40.** The Grinch/*How the Grinch Stole Christmas* (2000) **41.** Ernest/*Ernest Saves Christmas* (1988) **42.** Johnny/*Johnny English* (2003), *Johnny Handsome* (1989) **43.** *Primary Colors* (1998) **44.** *The Sum of All Fears* (2002) **45.** *The Color Purple* (1985) **46.** *The Hours* (2002) **47.** *25th Hour* (2002) **48.** *Mona Lisa* (1986) **49.** *Speechless* (1994) **50.** *What Lies Beneath* (2000).

14 ODD 1 OUT

1. (c) **2.** (d) **3.** (b) **4.** (a) – Antonio Banderas' character in *Play It to the Bone* (1999) **5.** (e) **6.** (c) **7.** (d) – A spin-off from *The Mummy* (1999) **8.** (b) **9.** (c) **10.** (d) **11.** (d) **12.** (d) **13.** (c) **14.** (b) **15.** (d) **16.** (d) **17.** (d) **18.** (c) **19.** (d) **20.** (b) **21.** (d) **22.** (a) **23.** (a) **24.** (e) – Lt. Comdr. Rick 'Jester' Heatherly **25.** (d) **26.** (c) **27.** (e) **28.** (e) **29.** (c) – Adam Sandler's character was only the Devil's son **30.** (f).

15 GUYS AND DOLLS

15.1 THE GUYS

1. ROBERT REDFORD: Debra Winger/*Legal Eagles* (1986), Lena Olin/*Havana* (1990), Mary McDonnell/*Sneakers* (1992), Jane Fonda/*The Electric Horseman* (1979) **2.** CHRISTIAN SLATER: Milla Jovovich/*Kuffs* (1992), Mary Stuart Masterson/*Bed of Roses* (1996), Winona Ryder/*Heathers* (1989), Samantha Mathis/*Broken Arrow* (1996) **3.** CHEVY CHASE: Sigourney Weaver/*Deal of the Century* (1983), Dianne Wiest/*Cops and Robbersons* (1994), Farrah Fawcett/*Man of the House* (1994), Daryl Hannah/*Memoirs of an Invisible Man* (1992) **4.** MICHAEL DOUGLAS: Geneviève Bujold/*Coma* (1978), Jill Clayburgh/*It's My Turn* (1980), Melanie Griffith/*Shining Through* (1992), Glenn Close/*Fatal Attraction* (1987) **5.** BRUCE WILLIS: Michelle Pfeiffer/*The Story of Us* (1999), Barbara Hershey/*Breakfast of Champions* (1999), Jane March/*Color of Night* (1994), Kim Basinger/*Blind Date* (1987) **6.** JACK NICHOLSON: Mary Steenburgen/*Goin' South* (1978), Ellen Barkin/*Man Trouble* (1992), Helen Hunt/*As Good As It Gets* (1997), Diane Keaton/*Something's Gotta Give* (2003) **7.** MATT DILLON: Sean Young/*A Kiss Before Dying* (1991), Nicole Kidman/*To Die For* (1995), Diane Lane/*The Big Town* (1987), Kelly Lynch/*Drugstore Cowboy* (1989).

15.2 THE DOLLS

1. HOLLY HUNTER: James Spader/*Crash* (1996), Richard Dreyfuss/*Always* (1989) and *Once Around* (1991), William Hurt/*Broadcast News* (1989), Harvey Keitel/*The Piano* (1993) **2.** SANDRA BULLOCK: Hugh Grant/*Two Weeks Notice* (2002), Ben Affleck/*Forces of Nature* (1999), Harry Connick Jr/*Hope Floats* (1998), Bill Pullman/*While You Were Sleeping* (1995) **3.** MARY ELIZABETH MASTRANTONIO: Willem Dafoe/*White Sands* (1992), Ed Harris/*The Abyss* (1989), Patrick Swayze/*Three Wishes* (1995), Al Pacino/*Two Bits* (1995) **4.** MEG RYAN: Matthew Broderick/*Addicted to Love* (1997), Val Kilmer/*The Doors* (1991), Kevin Kline/*French Kiss* (1995), Kiefer Sutherland/*Promised Land* (1987) **5.** ANDIE MACDOWELL: John Malkovich/*The Object of Beauty* (1991), Liam Neeson/*Ruby Cairo* (1993), Michael Keaton/*Multiplicity* (1996), Andy Garcia/*Just the Ticket* (1999) **6.** DEMI MOORE: Gary Oldman/*The Scarlet Letter* (1995), Michael Douglas/*Disclosure* (1994), Jeff Daniels/*The Butcher's Wife* (1991), Tom Cruise/*A Few Good Men* (1992) **7.** NASTASSJA KINSKI: Charlie Sheen/*Terminal Velocity* (1994), Dudley Moore/*Unfaithfully Yours* (1984), Ben Kingsley/*Harem* (1985), John Savage/*Maria's Lovers* (1984).

16 SIXES AND SEVENS

1. Harrison Ford, Gene Wilder/*The Frisco Kid* (1979), Charles Grodin/*The Woman in Red* (1984), Martin Short/*Clifford* (1994), Danny Glover/*Pure Luck* (1991), Willem Dafoe/*Flight of the Intruder* (1991), Harrison Ford/*Clear and Present Danger* (1994) **2.** Alec Baldwin, Meg Ryan/*Prelude to a Kiss* (1992), Kevin Spacey/*Hurlyburly* (1998), Andy Garcia/*A Show of Force* (1990), Kenneth Branagh/*Dead Again* (1991), Denzel Washington/*Much Ado About Nothing* (1993), Kelly Lynch/*Virtuosity* (1995), Alec Baldwin/*Heaven's Prisoners* (1996) **3.** Whoopi Goldberg, Elizabeth Perkins/*Moonlight and Valentino* (1995), Alan Arkin/*Indian Summer* (1993), Marisa Tomei/*Slums of Beverly Hills* (1998), Woody Harrelson/

Welcome to Sarajevo (1997), Kiefer Sutherland/*The Cowboy Way* (1994), Sally Field/*Eye for an Eye* (1996), Whoopi Goldberg/*Soapdish* (1991) **4.** John Travolta, Halle Berry/*Swordfish* (2001), Kurt Russell/*Executive Decision* (1996), Mel Gibson/*Tequila Sunrise* (1988), Jamie Lee Curtis/*Forever Young* (1992), Linda Fiorentino/*Queen's Logic* (1991), John Travolta/*Shout* (1991) **5.** Antonio Banderas, Emma Thompson/*Imagining Argentina* (2003), Jonathan Pryce/*Carrington* (1995), Madonna/*Evita* (1996), Harvey Keitel/*Dangerous Game* (1993), Theresa Russell/*Bad Timing* (1980), Jeremy Irons/*Kafka* (1991), Antonio Banderas/*The House of the Spirits* (1993) **6.** Kevin Kline, Rod Steiger/*The January Man* (1989), Charles Bronson/*Love and Bullets* (1979), Lee Marvin/*Death Hunt* (1981), William Hurt/*Gorky Park* (1983), Sigourney Weaver/*The Janitor* (1981), Kevin Kline/*Dave* (1993) and/or *The Ice Storm* (1997) **7.** John Cusack, Anjelica Huston/*The Grifters* (1990), Lena Olin/*Enemies: A Love Story* (1989), Claire Danes/*Polish Wedding* (1998), Matt Damon/*The Rainmaker* (1997), Charlize Theron/*The Legend of Bagger Vance* (2000), Al Pacino/*The Devil's Advocate* (1997), John Cusack/*City Hall* (1996) **8.** Ed Harris, Madeleine Stowe/*China Moon* (1994), Kevin Costner/*Revenge* (1990), Elijah Wood/*The War* (1994), Paul Hogan/*Flipper* (1996), Cuba Gooding Jr/*Lightning Jack* (1994), Anthony Hopkins/*Instinct* (1999), Ed Harris/*The Human Stain* (2003) and/or *Nixon* (1995) **9.** Albert Finney, Tom Courtenay/*The Dresser* (1983), Bob Hoskins/*Last Orders* (2001), Denzel Washington/*Heart Condition* (1990), Angelina Jolie/*The Bone Collector* (1999), David Duchovny/*Playing God* (1997), Julia Roberts/*Full Frontal* (2002), Albert Finney/*Erin Brockovich* (2000) **10.** Mel Gibson, Goldie Hawn/*Bird on a Wire* (1990), Geoffrey Rush/*The Banger Sisters* (2002), Kate Winslet/*Quills* (2000), Dougray Scott/*Enigma* (2001), Tim Roth/*To Kill a King* (2003), Mel Gibson/*The Million Dollar Hotel* (2000).

17 REMAKES

17.1 THE ORIGINALS

1. Steve McQueen (1968) **2.** Spencer Tracy (1950) **3.** Richard Roundtree (1971) **4.** Charlton Heston (1968) **5.** Rex Harrison (1967) **6.** Katharine Hepburn (1933) **7.** James Mason (1962) **8.** Audrey Hepburn (1954) **9.** Gena Rowlands (1980) **10.** Jack Benny (1942) **11.** Gregory Peck (1962) **12.** Cary Grant/*The Bishop's Wife* (1947) **13.** Ali MacGraw (1972) **14.** Don Ameche (1943) **15.** Anthony Newley (1968).

17.2 NEARLY NEW

1. *Sommersby* (1993) **2.** *City of Angels* (1998) **3.** *Breathless* (1983) **4.** *My Father the Hero* (1994) – Gérard Depardieu **5.** *Point Of No Return* (1994).

17.3 THE TRIVIA

1. Kazakhstan **2.** Instead of being just newspaper reporters they were cable TV news reporters. **3.** (c) **4.** *Psycho* (1960)/Every frame of the film, every scene and every camera angle were an exact copy of the original. **5.** Turin/Los Angeles **6.** *The Big Sleep* (1978)/It was located in England. **7.** (a) **8.** Midwich/*Village of the Damned* (1960)(1995) **9.** Miss Froy/*The Lady Vanishes* (1938)(1979) **10.** 3/Robert Donat (1935), Kenneth More (1959), Robert Powell (1978) **11.** *An Affair to Remember* (1957)/*Sleepless in Seattle* (1993) **12.** New York, because George (Jack Lemmon – (1970))/Henry (Steve Martin – (1999)) had a job interview. **13.** Sudan **14.** *A Perfect Murder* (1998) **15.** Hayley Mills **And finally . . .** Siam (Thailand)/*The King and I* (1956), *Anna and The King* (1999).

18 THE PLOT THICKENS

1. *Firefox* (1982) **2.** *The Cannonball Run* (1981) **3.** *Last Man Standing* (1996) **4.** *The Golden Child* (1986) **5.** *Chicken Run* (2000) **6.** *The Straight Story* (1999) **7.** *In & Out* (1997) **8.** *Zoolander* (2001) **9.** *The First Wives*

Club (1996) **10.** *Cool World* (1992) **11.** *The Great Train Robbery* (1979) **12.** *Air America* (1990) **13.** *The Boys from Brazil* (1978) **14.** *The Vanishing* (1993) **15.** *WarGames* (1983) **16.** *Finding Nemo* (2003) **17.** *Shadow of the Vampire* (2000) **18.** *Red Corner* (1997) **19.** *Being There* (1979) **20.** *Southern Comfort* (1981) **21.** *The Virgin Suicides* (1999) **22.** *Mississippi Burning* (1988) **23.** *Calendar Girls* (2003) **24.** *The Mosquito Coast* (1986) **25.** *The Pledge* (2001) **26.** *The Last Samurai* (2003) **27.** *Fame* (1980) **28.** *The Brylcreem Boys* (1999) **29.** *Shirley Valentine* (1989) **30.** *Blade II* (2002).

19 MIX UP

1. 1–5, 2–1, 3–4, 4–3, 5–2 **2.** 1–6, 2–7, 3–1, 4–3, 5–5, 6–4, 7–2/Michael Keaton in *Batman* (1989) and *Batman Returns* (1992), Val Kilmer in *Batman Forever* (1995), George Clooney in *Batman & Robin* (1997) **3.** 1–5, 2–4, 3–6, 4–1, 5–2, 6–3, 7–7 **4.** 1–2, 2–1, 3–3, 4–4, 5–5, 6–6 **5.** 1–2 *Red Heat* (1988), 2–3 *Sea of Love* (1989), 3–1 *Tango & Cash* (1989), 4–6 *Colors* (1988), 5–4 *The Corruptor* (1999), 6–5 *Running Scared* (1986) **6.** 1–6, 2–1, 3–2, 4–3, 5–4, 6–5 **7.** 1–1, 2–2, 3–4, 4–3, 5–5 **8.** 1–4, 2–1, 3–2, 4–6, 5–5, 6–3 **9.** 1–5, 2–1, 3–4, 4–3, 5–2 **10.** 1–5, 2–2, 3–4, 4–1, 5–3 **11.** 1–4, 2–7, 3–5, 4–6, 5–3, 6–1, 7–2 **12.** 1–3, 2–1, 3–6, 4–5, 5–2, 6–4 **13.** 1–2, 2–5, 3–4, 4–1, 5–3 **14.** 1–2, 2–4, 3–5, 4–1, 5–3 **15.** 1–2 *Dracula* (1992), 2–1 *Murder by Decree* (1979), 3–4 *Bruce Almighty* (2003), 4–3 *Greystoke: The Legend of Tarzan, Lord of the Apes* (1984), 5–5 *Robin Hood – Men in Tights* (1993) **16.** 1–3 *An Innocent Man* (1989), 2–1 *The Recruit* (2003), 3–2 *Wild Wild West* (1999), 4–6 *Stripes* (1981), 5–7 *Men of Honor* (2000), 6–4 *American History X* (1998), 7–5 *Copycat* (1995) **17.** 1–5/*Dunston Checks In* (1996), 2–2/*Paulie* (1998), 3–4/*Andre* (1994), 4–1/*Spirit – Stallion of the Cimarron* (2002), 5–3/*Cujo* (1983), 6–6/*Mighty Joe Young* (1998), 7–7/*Tarka the Otter* (1978) **18.** 1–3, 2–4, 3–5, 4–1, 5–2, 6–6, 7–7 **19.** 1–5, 2–1 or 2–4, 3–1 or 3–4, 4–3, 5–2 **20.** 1–6, 2–5, 3–4, 4–3, 5–2, 6–1.

20 THE NAME GAME 2 – THE DEFINITE ARTICLE

1. Adam Sandler **2.** Charlize Theron **3.** Robert Redford **4.** Kevin Costner **5.** Meryl Streep **6.** Adrien Brody **7.** Bill Murray **8.** Charlie Sheen **9.** Robin Wright Penn **10.** Chris O'Donnell **11.** Eddie Murphy **12.** Robert Duvall **13.** Steve Martin **14.** Peter Falk **15.** Terence Stamp **16.** Robert Mitchum **17.** Christopher Reeve **18.** Richard Pryor **19.** Denzel Washington **20.** Jet Li **21.** John Goodman **22.** Sylvester Stallone **23.** Joan Allen **24.** Billy Zane **25.** Burt Reynolds **26.** Rutger Hauer **27.** Lara Flynn Boyle **28.** Robert Duvall **29.** Faye Dunaway **30.** Geoffrey Rush.

21 WHERE WAS WHERE

21.1 HOLLYWOOD ABROAD

1. Indonesia **2.** France **3.** Kenya **4.** Scotland **5.** Ireland **6.** South Africa **7.** Italy **8.** India **9.** Austria **10.** Greece.

21.2 BRIGHT LIGHTS, BIG CITY

1. Baltimore **2.** San Francisco **3.** Los Angeles **4.** New York **5.** Detroit **6.** Las Vegas **7.** Miami **8.** Philadelphia **9.** New Orleans **10.** Boston.

21.3 ONLY IN THE MOVIES

1. *The Truman Show* (1998) **2.** *Gremlins* (1984–90) **3.** *Shrek* (2001) **4.** *The Nightmare Before Christmas* (1993) **5.** *How the Grinch Stole Christmas* (2000) **6.** *The Fog* (1980) **7.** *Mystery Men* (1999) **8.** *Demolition Man* (1993) **9.** *Cookie's Fortune* (1999) **10.** *Tremors* (1990) **11.** *Grease* (1978–82) **12.** *Hairspray* (1988) **13.** *Taps* (1981) **14.** *Being John Malkovich* (1999) **15.** *Brubaker* (1980) **16.** *The Ballad of the Sad Café* (1991) **17.** *Crimson Tide* (1995) **18.** *Dangerous Minds* (1995) **19.** *The Mummy* (1999) **20.** *Scooby Doo* (2002) **21.** *Four Rooms* (1995) **22.** *From Dusk Till Dawn* (1996) **23.** *The 'Burbs* (1989) **24.** *Die Hard* (1988) **25.** *Friday 13th* (1980)

26. *Indiana Jones and the Temple of Doom* (1984) **27.** *Top Secret!* (1984) **28.** *Hot Shots!* (1991) **29.** *Ghost Ship* (2002) **30.** *Girl, Interrupted* (1999).

22 DEBUTS
22.1 OUT FRONT

1. Kate Winslet **2.** Eddie Murphy **3.** Denzel Washington **4.** William Hurt **5.** Ashley Judd **6.** Meg Ryan **7.** Halle Berry **8.** Jennifer Jason Leigh **9.** Winona Ryder **10.** Emma Thompson.

22.2 BEHIND THE CAMERA

1. Anthony Minghella **2.** John Singleton **3.** Nora Ephron **4.** Barry Levinson **5.** Michael Caton-Jones **6.** Danny Boyle **7.** Simon West **8.** John Dahl **9.** Kevin Smith **10.** Jan De Bont.

22.3 REVERSAL OF FORTUNE

1. Mel Gibson **2.** Robert De Niro **3.** Edward Norton **4.** Kevin Spacey **5.** Jodie Foster **6.** Tim Robbins **7.** Morgan Freeman **8.** Emilio Estevez **9.** Anthony Hopkins **10.** John Turturro.

23 THE FILMOGRAPHY
23.1 THE C.V.

1. ROBIN WILLIAMS: *Jakob the Liar* (1999), *The Birdcage* (1996), *Cadillac Man* (1990), *Toys* (1992), *Popeye* (1980) **2.** SEAN CONNERY: *The Hunt for Red October* (1990), *Highlander* (1986), *The Name of the Rose* (1986), *Finding Forrester* (2000), *First Knight* (1995) **3.** ALEC BALDWIN: *Talk Radio* (1988), *Miami Blues* (1990), *The Edge* (1997), *The Marrying Man* (1991), *The Shadow* (1994) **4.** TOM HANKS: *Punchline* (1988), *Volunteers* (1985),

The Green Mile (1999), *A League of Their Own* (1992), *Toy Story* (1995–99)
5. JEFF BRIDGES: *Tucker – The Man and His Dream* (1988), *The Fisher King* (1991), *Starman* (1984), *Fearless* (1993), *Wild Bill* (1995) **6.** MICHELLE PFEIFFER: *Grease 2* (1982), *The Fabulous Baker Boys* (1989), *Up Close & Personal* (1996), *Love Field* (1992), *A Midsummer Night's Dream* (1999) **7.** WILLEM DAFOE: *Triumph of the Spirit* (1989), *Edges of the Lord* (2001), *Streets of Fire* (1984), *Tom & Viv* (1994), *The Last Temptation of Christ* (1988) **8.** WOODY ALLEN: *The Curse of the Jade Scorpion* (2001), *Small Time Crooks* (2000), *Picking Up the Pieces* (2000), *Zelig* (1983), *Antz* (1998) **9.** EDDIE MURPHY: *Boomerang* (1992), *A Vampire in Brooklyn* (1995), *The Golden Child* (1985), *Coming to America* (1988), *Shrek* (2001–04) **10.** MICHAEL CAINE: *Shiner* (2000), *Little Voice* (1998), *Educating Rita* (1983), *On Deadly Ground* (1994), *Without a Clue* (1988).

23.2 THE THREESOME

1. Morgan Freeman **2.** Uma Thurman **3.** Ralph Fiennes **4.** Melanie Griffith **5.** Andy Garcia **6.** Kim Basinger **7.** Ellen Barkin **8.** William Hurt **9.** Jeff Daniels **10.** Brad Pitt.

23.3 THE ONE

1. *Junior* (1994) **2.** *Larger Than Life* (1996) **3.** *Sphere* (1998) **4.** *Ruthless People* (1986) **5.** *The Patriot* (2000) **6.** *A Simple Plan* (1998) **7.** *Wolf* (1994) **8.** *Private Benjamin* (1980) **9.** *Anaconda* (1997) **10.** *Honkytonk Man* (1982) **11.** *The 51st State* (2001) **12.** *North* (1994) **13.** *Shallow Hal* (2001) **14.** *Blast from the Past* (1999) **15.** *Eddie* (1996).

23.4 THE OBSCURE

1. *King Ralph* (1991) **2.** *Lassiter* (1984) **3.** *Time After Time* (1979) **4.** *Give My Regards to Broad Street* (1984) **5.** *Oh! Heavenly Dog* (1980) **6.** *Lion of the Desert* (1980) **7.** *The Awakening* (1980) **8.** *S.O.B.* (1981) **9.** *Duet for One*

(1986) **10.** *Q – The Winged Serpent* (1982) **11.** *Rough Cut* (1980) **12.** *Hooper* (1978) **13.** *Paternity* (1981) **14.** *Cop and a Half* (1993) **15.** *Rent-a-Cop* (1988).

23.5 THE GAPS

1. *Cutthroat Island* (1995) **2.** *The Others* (2001) **3.** *Othello* (1995) **4.** *Lorenzo's Oil* (1992) **5.** *Under Fire* (1983) **6.** *Dead Man Walking* (1995) **7.** *Quick Change* (1990) **8.** *Cocktail* (1988) **9.** *Rob Roy* (1995) **10.** *Black Widow* (1987).

23.6 THE END BIT

1. YES **2.** YES **3.** YES **4.** YES **5.** NO/Julia Stiles **6.** YES **7.** NO/Sarah Jessica Parker **8.** NO/Joely Richardson **9.** YES **10.** YES **11.** YES **12.** NO/Helena Bonham Carter **13.** YES **14.** NO/Laura Linney **15.** NO/Sarah Michelle Gellar **16.** YES **17.** YES **18.** NO/Daniel Day Lewis **19.** NO/Scott Glenn **20.** YES.

24 CHARACTER STUDY

24.1 NAMING NAMES

1. Arnold Schwarzenegger in *Last Action Hero* (1993) **2.** Kathleen Turner in *Romancing the Stone* (1984), *The Jewel of the Nile* (1985) **3.** Mike Myers in *Wayne's World* (1992–93) **4.** Jeff Goldblum in *The Fly* (1986) **5.** Nicolas Cage in *Face/Off* (1997) **6.** Vin Diesel in *xXx* (2002–05) **7.** Woody Allen in *Manhattan* (1979) **8.** Whoopi Goldberg in *Corrina, Corrina* (1994) **9.** Jim Carrey in *Ace Ventura – Pet Detective* (1994), *Ace Ventura – When Nature Calls* (1995) **10.** Clint Eastwood in *Unforgiven* (1992) **11.** Robert Redford in *The Natural* (1984) **12.** Joe Pesci in *Jimmy Hollywood* (1994) **13.** Robin Williams in *Mrs Doubtfire* (1993) **14.** Michelle Pfeiffer in *The Fabulous Baker Boys* (1989) **15.** Cher in *Mermaids* (1990) **16.** Jack Nicholson in *Anger Management* (2003) **17.** Alicia Silverstone in *Clueless* (1995)

18. James Caan in *Misery* (1990) **19.** Neve Campbell in *Scream* (1996–2000) **20.** Steve Martin in *The Man with Two Brains* (1983) **21.** Glenn Close in *Fatal Attraction* (1987) **22.** John Cusack in *Grosse Point Blank* (1997) **23.** Charles Bronson in *Death Wish* (1974–94) **24.** Frances McDormand in *Fargo* (1996) **25.** Al Pacino in *Carlito's Way* (1993) **26.** Robert De Niro in *The King of Comedy* (1983) **27.** Johnny Depp in *What's Eating Gilbert Grape?* (1993) **28.** Angelina Jolie in *Lara Croft: Tomb Raider* (2001–03) **29.** Dan Aykroyd in *The Blues Brothers* (1980–98) **30.** Val Kilmer in *The Saint* (1997).

24.2 THE PERSONALITIES

1. Dr Robert Elliott (Michael Caine) in *Dressed to Kill* (1980) **2.** Elena Montero (Catherine Zeta-Jones) in *The Mask of Zorro* (1998) **3.** Dickie Greenleaf (Jude Law) in *The Talented Mr Ripley* (1999) **4.** Mark Hunter, aka Hard Harry (Christian Slater) in *Pump Up the Volume* (1990) **5.** Brandy, aka Rollergirl (Heather Graham) in *Boogie Nights* (1997) **6.** Alex Owens (Jennifer Beals) in *Flashdance* (1983) **7.** Patrick Bateman (Christian Bale) in *American Psycho* (2000) **8.** Ronny Cammareri (Nicolas Cage) in *Moonstruck* (1987) **9.** Chuck Barris (Sam Rockwell) in *Confessions of a Dangerous Mind* (2002) **10.** Matt Murdock, aka Daredevil (Ben Affleck) in *Daredevil* (2003).

24.3 IT'S A LIVING

1. Judge **2.** Boat Builder **3.** Politician **4.** Lawyer **5.** Architect **6.** Dustman **7.** Firefighter **8.** Shopkeeper **9.** Prostitute **10.** Jockey.

24.4 THE VOICE TALENT

1. Kevin Bacon **2.** Cameron Diaz **3.** Meg Ryan **4.** Joan Cusack **5.** Robin Williams **6.** Demi Moore **7.** Matthew Broderick **8.** Minnie Driver **9.** Eddie Murphy **10.** Val Kilmer.

24.5 THE BACK CATALOGUE

1. JOHN TRAVOLTA/*Saturday Night Fever* (1977) and *Staying Alive* (1983), *Swordfish* (2001), *Get Shorty* (1995), *Grease* (1978) **2.** TOM CRUISE/*Mission Impossible* (1996–2005), *The Firm* (1993), *Born on the Fourth of July* (1989), *Interview with the Vampire – The Vampire Chronicles* (1994) **3.** JULIA ROBERTS/*Pretty Woman* (1990), *Mary Reilly* (1996), *The Pelican Brief* (1993), *Mona Lisa Smile* (2003) **4.** HARRISON FORD/*Regarding Henry* (1991), *Working Girl* (1988), *Hollywood Homicide* (2003), *The Fugitive* (1993) **5.** KEVIN COSTNER/*Bull Durham* (1988), *The Bodyguard* (1992), *JFK* (1991), *Open Range* (2003) **6.** RICHARD GERE/*The Cotton Club* (1984), *Pretty Woman* (1990), *An Officer and a Gentleman* (1982), *American Gigolo* (1980) **7.** EDDIE MURPHY/*Trading Places* (1983), *48 Hrs.* (1982) and *Another 48 Hrs.* (1990), *Beverly Hills Cop* (1984–94), *The Nutty Professor* (1996–2000).

24.6 THE CAST LIST

1. *Snatch* (2000) **2.** *Dick Tracy* (1990) **3.** *Once Upon a Time in America* (1984) **4.** *American Pie* (1999) **5.** *Time Bandits* (1981) **6.** *Kill Bill* (2003) **7.** *The League of Extraordinary Gentlemen* (2003) **8.** *The Goonies* (1985) **9.** *Alien* (1979) **10.** *St. Elmo's Fire* (1985).

25 5 × 5
25.1 THE GIMMICKS

1. *eXistenZ* **2.** *Se7en* **3.** *Jungle 2 Jungle* **4.** *Thir13en Ghosts* **5.** *S1m0ne*.

25.2 TWICE AROUND

1. *Red Planet* (2000) **2.** *A Bug's Life* (1998) **3.** *Tombstone* (1994) **4.** *1492 – Conquest of Paradise* (1992) **5.** *Photographing Fairies* (1997).

25.3 THE ALTERNATIVE TITLE

1. *X-Men 2* (2003) **2.** *Mission Impossible 2* (2000) **3.** *The League of Extraordinary Gentlemen* (2003) **4.** *Independence Day* (1996) **5.** *Men in Black II* (2002).

25.4 THE COLOUR SCHEME OF THINGS

1. Pink/*Pink Cadillac* (1989) **2.** White/*White Oleander* (2002) **3.** Red/*Red Dawn* (1984) **4.** Blue/*Blue Chips* (1994) **5.** Black/*Black Robe* (1991).

25.5 WHAT MIGHT HAVE BEEN

1. *Cabin Fever* (2003) **2.** *They* (2002) **3.** *Tall Tale* (1995) **4.** *Labyrinth* (1986) **5.** *The Crow* (1994–2004).

26 SMART TALK 2

1. *Roxanne* (1987)/A = Steve Martin (C.D. Bales), B = Daryl Hannah (Roxanne Kowalski) **2.** *Airplane* (1980)/A = Robert Hays (Ted Striker), B = Julie Hagerty (Elaine Dickinson) **3.** *The Elephant Man* (1980)/A = John Hurt (John Merrick), B = Anthony Hopkins (Dr Frederick Treves) **4.** *Thief* (1981)/A = Hal Frank (Joe Gags), B = James Caan (Frank) **5.** *Showtime* (2002)/A = William Shatner (William Shatner), B = Robert De Niro (Det. Mitch Preston) **6.** *Dumb & Dumber* (1994)/A = Jim Carrey (Lloyd Christmas), B = Jeff Daniels (Harry Dunne) **7.** *Big* (1988)/A = Elizabeth Perkins (Susan), B = Tom Hanks (Josh Baskin) **8.** *Terms of Endearment* (1983)/A = Shirley MacLaine (Aurora Greenway), B = Jack Nicholson (Garrett Breedlove) **9.** *Kingpin* (1996)/A = Vanessa Angel (Claudia), B = Woody Harrelson (Roy Munson) **10.** *Dead Men Don't Wear Plaid* (1982)/ A = Rachel Ward (Juliet Forrest), B = Steve Martin (Rigby Reardon) **11.** *Witness* (1985)/A = Kelly McGillis (Rachel Lapp), B = Jan Rubes (Eli Lapp) **12.** *Urban Cowboy* (1980)/A = Debra Winger (Sissy Davis), B = John Travolta ('Bud' Davis) **13.** *Tootsie* (1982)/A = Dustin Hoffman (Michael

Dorsey), B = Sydney Pollack (George Fields) **14.** *Pulp Fiction* (1994)/A = Eric Stoltz (Lance), B = John Travolta (Vincent Vega) **15.** *Field of Dreams* (1989)/A = Ray Liotta (Shoeless Joe Jackson), B = Kevin Costner (Ray Kinsella) **16.** *Fried Green Tomatoes* (1991)/A = Jessica Tandy (Ninny Threadgoode), B = Kathy Bates (Evelyn Couch) **17.** *Speed* (1994)/A = Dennis Hopper (Howard Payne), B = Keanu Reeves (Jack Traven) **18.** *Clue* (1985)/A = Madeline Kahn (Mrs White), B = Lesley Ann Warren (Miss Scarlett), C = Tim Curry (Wadsworth) **19.** *Cocoon* (1985)/A = Hume Cronyn (Joseph Finley), B = Wilford Brimley (Ben Luckett), C = Don Ameche (Art Selwyn) **20.** *Yentl* (1983)/A = Barbra Streisand (Yentl), B = Nehemiah Persoff (Yentl's Father).

27 BODY PARTS 2

27.1 THE NUMBERS

1. *Bat-21* (1988) **2.** *Girl 6* (1996) **3.** *8 Heads in a Duffel Bag* (1997) **4.** *Code 46* (2003) **5.** *15 Minutes* (2001) **6.** *Murder at 1600* (1997) **7.** *Passenger 57* (1992) **8.** *8 Million Ways to Die* (1986) **9.** *200 Cigarettes* (1999) **10.** *U-571* (2000) **11.** *10 Things I Hate About You* (1999) **12.** *Jennifer 8* (1992) **13.** *2 Days in The Valley* (1996) **14.** *Roadhouse 66* (1984) **15.** *13 Conversations About One Thing* (2001) **16.** *Track 29* (1988) **17.** *Buffalo 66* (1998) **18.** *3000 Miles to Graceland* (2001) **19.** *3 AM* (2001) **20.** *84 Charing Cross Road* (1987) **21.** *Love Potion #9* (1992) **22.** *52 Pick Up* (1986) **23.** *Transylvania 6-5000* (1985) **24.** *Article 99* (1992) **25.** *Session 9* (2001).

27.2 THE MATHS

1. $3 + 10 =$ *Apollo 13* (1995) **2.** $57 - 52 + 3 =$ *8MM* (1999) **3.** $46 + 8 =$ *Car 54 Where Are You?* (1994) **4.** $84 - 46 - 29 - 2 =$ *Seven Years in Tibet* (1997) **5.** $66 - 46 - 10 =$ *How to Lose a Guy in 10 Days* (2003) **6.** $3000/3/10 + 2 =$ *102 Dalmatians* (2000) **7.** $21 - 9 - 2 =$ *10* (1979).

28 ODD 1 IN

1. (b) **2.** (c) **3.** (d) **4.** (a) **5.** (c) **6.** (b) **7.** (a) **8.** (b) **9.** (e) **10.** (d) **11.** (a) **12.** (b) **13.** (b) **14.** (b) **15.** (c) **16.** (b) **17.** (d) **18.** (c) **19.** (a) **20.** (b).

29 TWO OF A KIND

1. Al Pacino **2.** Robin Williams **3.** Thora Birch **4.** Julia Stiles **5.** Owen Wilson **6.** Ray Liotta **7.** Sean Young **8.** Bill Paxton **9.** Tom Hanks **10.** Harrison Ford **11.** Gene Hackman **12.** Paul Newman **13.** Burt Lancaster **14.** Helen Hunt **15.** Meg Ryan **16.** Cameron Diaz **17.** Drew Barrymore **18.** Demi Moore **19.** Diane Keaton **20.** Penélope Cruz **21.** George Clooney **22.** Steven Seagal **23.** Nick Nolte **24.** Rick Moranis **25.** Robert Downey Jr **26.** Leonardo Di Caprio **27.** Kevin Spacey **28.** Steve Buscemi **29.** Chevy Chase **30.** Jason Patric **31.** Jeremy Irons **32.** Antonio Banderas **33.** Ben Stiller **34.** Martin Lawrence **35.** Denzel Washington **36.** Marlon Brando **37.** Philip Seymour Hoffman **38.** Val Kilmer **39.** Madonna **40.** David Niven **41.** Bette Davis **42.** J.T. Walsh **43.** Sam Elliott **44.** Eric Stoltz **45.** Harry Dean Stanton **46.** Chris O'Donnell **47.** Ice T **48.** Colin Farrell **49.** Ryan O'Neal **50.** Steve Guttenberg **51.** Charlie Sheen **52.** Alicia Silverstone **53.** Chazz Palminteri **54.** Liam Neeson **55.** John Gielgud **56.** Ralph Fiennes **57.** Patricia Arquette **58.** Christopher Walken **59.** Liza Minnelli **60.** John Candy.

30 JAMES BOND

1. Ian Fleming **2.** 20 **3.** Sean Connery (1962–71), George Lazenby (1969), Roger Moore (1973–85), Timothy Dalton (1987–89), Pierce Brosnan (1995–) and David Niven in *Casino Royale* (1967) **4.** (a) – Roger Moore (1985), (b) – Pierce Brosnan (2002), (c) – Sean Connery (1967), (d) – Sean Connery (1962), (e) – Roger Moore (1981) **5.** *On Her Majesty's Secret Service* (1969) **6.** *Thunderball* (1965) **7.** *Licence to Kill* (1989) **8.** **Sp**ecial **E**xecutive for **C**ounter Intelligence, **T**errorism, **R**evenge and **E**xtortion

9. *Thunderball* (1965)/Best Visual Effects **10.** 007/*Goldfinger* (1964) **11.** A fold-away helicopter/*You Only Live Twice* (1967) **12.** *Diamonds Are Forever* (1971) **13.** Joe Don Baker **14.** Shirley Bassey/*Goldfinger* (1964), *Diamonds Are Forever* (1971), *Moonraker* (1978) **15.** *For Your Eyes Only* (1981) **16.** (a) **17.** It was amphibious. **18.** (b) **19.** *Goldfinger* (1964) **20.** Major Geoffrey Boothroyd **21.** (a) — Gustav Graves (Toby Stephens) in *Die Another Day* (2002), (b) — Hugo Drax (Michael Lonsdale) in *Moonraker* (1979), (c) — Elliot Carver (Jonathan Pryce) in *Tomorrow Never Dies* (1997) **22.** (a) — *A View to a Kill* (1985), (b) — *From Russia with Love* (1963), (c) — *The Spy Who Loved Me* (1977) **23.** A CIA agent — By being fed to the sharks by Franz Sanchez (Robert Davi)/*Licence to Kill* (1989) **24.** (a) — *Diamonds Are Forever* (1971), (b) — *The Spy Who Loved Me* (1977) and *Moonraker* (1979), (c) — *The Man with the Golden Gun* (1974), (d) — *Goldfinger* (1964), (e) — *Live and Let Die* (1973). Jaws found true love in *Moonraker* (1979) **25.** Universal Exports **And finally . . .** *The World Is Not Enough* (1999).

31 BITS AND PIECES

1. The Commitments/*The Commitments* (1991) **2.** *Cinderella* **3.** *Jackie Brown* (1997) and *Out of Sight* (1998) **4.** *Ladyhawke* (1985) **5.** Halle Berry/*Losing Isaiah* (1995) **6.** *Monsters, Inc.* (2001) **7.** *Ocean's Eleven* (2001) **8.** Frank Sinatra **9.** *Three Amigos* (1986) **10.** 'Copland'/*Copland* (1997) **11.** *I'll Do Anything* (1994) **12.** Judi Dench — Elizabeth I in *Shakespeare in Love* (1998) and Victoria in *Mrs Brown* (1997) **13.** Kathleen Turner/*Who Framed Roger Rabbit?* (1988) **14.** A pseudonym used by Robin Williams in *The Adventures of Baron Munchausen* (1988) **15.** Burt Lancaster and Kirk Douglas/*Tough Guys* (1986) **16.** Tom Hanks **17.** Spider-Man/*Spider-Man* (2002) **18.** *A Shot at Glory* (2000) **19.** Nothing. He adopted the middle initial 'J' as a tribute to character actor, Michael J. Pollard **20.** Drew Barrymore **21.** Albert Brooks **22.** TriBeCa **23.** *Scary*

Movie **24.** *Hudson Hawk* (1991)/They were all names of supporting characters. **25.** *Habeas Corpus*, the film-within-a-film in *The Player* (1992) **26.** *All That Jazz* (1979) **27.** *Fierce Creatures* (1997) **28.** *She's Having a Baby* (1988) **29.** Mr Blonde (Vic Vega) **30.** *Toy Story* (1995).

32 DIRECTOR'S CUT

32.1 THE BACK CATALOGUE

1. Joel Shumacher **2.** William Friedkin **3.** Tony Scott **4.** Roman Polanski **5.** Bill Forsyth **6.** Alan Parker **7.** Rob Reiner **8.** Peter Weir **9.** Jonathan Lynn **10.** Lawrence Kasdan **11.** Ang Lee **12.** Paul Verhoeven **13.** Ridley Scott **14.** Jane Campion **15.** Jonathan Demme **16.** Norman Jewison **17.** Milos Foreman **18.** Renny Harlin **19.** Neil Jordan **20.** John Schlesinger.

32.2 TWO OF A KIND

1. Wes Craven **2.** Paul Thomas Anderson **3.** David Lean **4.** John Waters **5.** John McTiernan **6.** Steven Spielberg **7.** Penny Marshall **8.** David Lynch **9.** John Hughes **10.** John Landis **11.** Alan J. Pakula **12.** Francis Ford Coppola **13.** Oliver Stone **14.** Stanley Kubrick **15.** Whit Stillman **16.** Adrian Lynne **17.** Ken Loach.

32.3 THE TRIVIA

1. Woody Allen, Francis Ford Coppola and Martin Scorsese **2.** *Hope and Glory* (1987) **3.** Johnny Depp – *Plan 9 from Outer Space* (1959) **4.** *Lost in La Mancha* (2002) **5.** Vincent Van Gogh **6.** *White Hunter, Black Heart* (1990) **7.** Frank Oz **8.** Steven Spielberg/*Austin Powers in Goldmember* (2002) **9.** James Ivory (Director), Ismail Merchant (Producer) **10.** *Close Encounters of the Third Kind* (1977) (1980) **And finally . . .** Alan Smithee.

33 FAMILY TIES

33.1 ONLY IN THE MOVIES

1. Mary Steenburgen **2.** Meg Ryan **3.** Matt Dillon **4.** Sissy Spacek **5.** Shirley MacLaine **6.** William Baldwin **7.** Anthony Hopkins **8.** Matt Damon **9.** Mary Stuart Masterson **10.** Marisa Tomei **11.** Michael Keaton **12.** Anna Paquin **13.** Jessica Lange **14.** Bruno Kirby **15.** Teà Leoni **16.** Kyra Sedgwick **17.** Chevy Chase **18.** James Caan **19.** Woody Harrelson **20.** Annabella Sciorra **21.** Hume Cronyn **22.** Armin Muller-Stahl **23.** Maureen O'Hara **24.** Matthew Broderick **25.** Susan Sarandon **26.** Nicolas Cage **27.** Jennifer Love Hewitt **28.** Demi Moore **29.** Mary Elizabeth Mastrantonio **30.** Bruce Willis.

33.2 REAL LIFE

1. ERIC ROBERTS/Julia Roberts **2.** NATASHA RICHARDSON/Michael Redgrave, Vanessa Redgrave, Joely Richardson, Liam Neeson **3.** JOAQUIN PHOENIX (ex-Leaf Phoenix)/River Phoenix, Rain Phoenix **4.** DREW BARRY-MORE/John Drew Barrymore, Ethel and Lionel Barrymore, John Barrymore, Steven Spielberg **5.** WARREN BEATTY/Shirley MacLaine, Annette Bening **6.** KEITH CARRADINE/John Carradine, David Carradine, Martha Plimpton **7.** ALEC BALDWIN/Kim Basinger, William Baldwin, Stephen Baldwin, Daniel Baldwin **8.** JANE FONDA/Bridget Fonda, Peter Fonda, Henry Fonda **9.** SEAN PENN/Leo Penn, Chris Penn, Robin Wright-Penn, Madonna **10.** FRANCIS FORD COPPOLA/Carmine Coppola, Talia Shire, Nicolas Cage, Sophia Coppola.

34 OSCAR

34.1 THE FILMS

1. $5,000 **2.** Princeton **3.** Germania (Germany) **4.** Frank Fitts, the next door neighbour **5.** Romeo and Ethel, The Pirate's Daughter **6.** The White

Star Line **7.** Hungarian **8.** Edward I **9.** John Lennon **10.** Red **11.** Big Whiskey, WY **12.** Buffalo Bill **13.** Two Socks **14.** Miss Daisy's son, Boolie (Dan Aykroyd) **15.** Peoples' Court **16.** China **17.** 25th Infantry **18.** Coffee **19.** Emperor Joseph II **20.** Astronaut **21.** Lawyer **22.** 1924, Paris Olympics **23.** In a boating accident. **24.** To fight each other for custody of their son, Billy (Justin Henry). **25.** Russian Roulette.

34.2 THE TRIVIA

1. *Shrek* (2001) **2.** *Silence of the Lambs* (1991) **3.** Linda Hunt/*The Year of Living Dangerously* (1982) **4.** Marlon Brando/*The Godfather* (1971) **5.** *Midnight Cowboy* (1969) **6.** Roberto Benigni/*La Vita è Bella (Life Is Beautiful)* (1997) **7.** *The Lion in Winter* (1968) and *Funny Girl* (1968) **8.** *Cimarron* (1931) and *Dances with Wolves* (1991) **9.** John Ford **10.** *The Untouchables* (1987) **11.** *City Slickers* (1991) **12.** *The Godfather Part II* (1974) **13.** At 5½ – 6 minutes long, it is still thought of as the longest 'victory' speech in Oscar history/*Mrs Miniver* (1942) **14.** Both awards went to African-Americans for the first time/Denzel Washington (*Training Day* (2001)) and Halle Berry (*Monster's Ball* (2001)) **15.** (a)/The 25th Academy Awards **And finally . . .** Maggie Smith/*California Suite* (1978). Her character was that of an Oscar nominee who doesn't win the coveted gold statue; a role for which she herself won an Academy Award.

34.3 THE WINNERS

1. Angelina Jolie **2.** James Coburn **3.** Daniel Day Lewis **4.** Sissy Spacek **5.** Mary Steenburgen **6.** Robert Duvall **7.** Hilary Swank **8.** Jim Broadbent **9.** Geoffrey Rush **10.** Mira Sorvino **11.** Michael Caine **12.** Sally Field **13.** Sally Field **14.** Jeremy Irons **15.** Mercedes Ruehl **16.** William Hurt **17.** Maureen Stapleton **18.** Jon Voight **19.** Jason Robards **20.** Geraldine Page.

35 SPECIFICS

1. *Andrea Gail* **2.** Doctor Bronx **3.** 88 mph **4.** On a $5 bill **5.** $4,000,000 **6.** The Shop Around The Corner **7.** *Badge of Honor* **8.** Jack Rabbit Slim's (a kitschy 1950s themed restaurant) **9.** The Americans **10.** Norman **11.** Iowa **12.** Hair gel **13.** Platform 9¾ **14.** Turbo Man **15.** Fatso, Stinkie and Stretch **16.** Super Six One – Mogadishu **17.** General George Armstrong Custer **18.** 4 – 4 **19.** 7 days **20.** 5 **21.** Norway **22.** Always Be Closing **23.** A Kangaroo **24.** $200 **25.** Project Destiny **26.** Independence and Freedom **27.** Harrier Jump Jet **28.** C.R.S. (Consumer Recreation Services) **29.** $20,000 **30.** Serial killing murder sites **31.** Buenos Aires **32.** His dead wife, Rheya (Natascha McElhone) **33.** Io **34.** The Rumble In The Jungle **35.** Roger Smith, CEO General Motors **36.** Carnegie Hall, NYC **37.** From Russia With Love **38.** 12 **39.** Hot Metal **40.** Fort Henry **41.** D'Artagnan **42.** Brazil **43.** Scrat **44.** The Sorcerer's Apprentice **45.** Harryhausen's Sushi Bar **46.** Raymond Avila (Andy Garcia) was investigating Dennis Peck (Richard Gere) **47.** By pretending to be a telephone repair man **48.** Sour milk.

36 TRUE OR FALSE

1. FALSE/Strange Fruit **2.** FALSE/Rhino **3.** FALSE/Baboon's heart **4.** TRUE **5.** FALSE/His missing wife **6.** FALSE/Miss New Jersey **7.** TRUE **8.** TRUE **9.** FALSE/He was searching for his sister on K2 **10.** TRUE **11.** FALSE/Ice Hockey **12.** TRUE **13.** TRUE **14.** TRUE **15.** FALSE/Shoe shop **16.** FALSE/Brooklyn Bridge **17.** FALSE/Robot #5 **18.** TRUE **19.** FALSE/She suspected the murdered woman's husband **20.** TRUE **21.** TRUE **22.** FALSE/Mercury Space Program **23.** FALSE/All things Italian **24.** TRUE **25.** FALSE/Texas **26.** TRUE **27.** TRUE **28.** FALSE/*Rolling Stone* magazine **29.** TRUE **30.** TRUE.

37 BEHIND THE SCENES
37.1 THE WRITERS
1. Lowell Ganz and Babaloo Mandel **2.** Shane Black **3.** Joe Esterhaus **4.** David Mamet **5.** Eric Roth.

37.2 THE PRODUCERS
1. Joel Silver **2.** Jerry Bruckheimer **3.** Lili Fini Zanuck and Richard D. Zanuck **4.** Scott Rudin **5.** Saul Zaentz.

37.3 THE MUSICIANS
1. John Williams **2.** Hans Zimmer **3.** Howard Shore **4.** Thomas Newman **5.** Jerry Goldsmith.

37.4 THE TECHNICAL SUPPORT
1. The Chief Electrician **2.** The Gaffer's Assistant **3.** Sound Effects (The Creaking Door, Footsteps, etc.) **4.** The people responsible for trees, plants and all things horticultural (real or artificial) that may be needed on a film set. **5.** The team that sets up and dismantles a set.

37.5 THE BIZ
1. 24 f.p.s. **2.** Art For Art's Sake **3.** Western **4.** 2.2:1 **5.** **I**mage **Max**imisation **6.** Steven Spielberg, Jeffrey Katzenberg and David Geffen **7.** The Warner Brothers/Founders of the Warner Bros. studios in 1923 **8.** Sony owns Columbia Pictures **9.** **Ext**erior scene **10.** **M**otion **P**icture **A**ssociation of **A**merica.

38 THE END REEL
1. Christopher Walken **2.** Mr Creosote **3.** *Charlie's Angels* (2000) **4.** *Eight Men Out* (1988) **5.** The Widowmaker/*K19: The Widowmaker* (2002) **6.** Cindy

Crawford **7.** Arnold Schwarzenegger/*Kindergarten Cop* (1990) **8.** *Once Upon a Time in Mexico* (2003)/#1 – *El Mariachi* (1992), #2 – *Desperado* (1995) **9.** Walter 'Gib' Gibson (John Cusack)/*The Sure Thing* (1985) **10.** *The Hunger* (1983) **11.** *Feds* (1988) **12.** The Firm/*The Firm* (1993) **13.** Veronica Lake **14.** Virginia Hill **15.** Kevin Bacon **16.** *House of the Long Shadows* (1983) **17.** Cambodia **18.** Jupiter 2/*Lost in Space* (1998) **19.** 6/*Cube* (1997) **20.** Crepe Suzette **21.** *Capricorn One* (1979) **22.** *Rumble Fish* (1983) **23.** Snake Eyes/*Snake Eyes* (1998) **24.** Piglet/*Piglet's Big Movie* (2003) **25.** *Jack Frost* (1998) **26.** Anthony Hopkins/*The Bounty* (1984) **27.** Debbie Jellinsky (Joan Cusack)/*Addams Family Values* (1993) **28.** On the Moon/*The Adventures of Pluto Nash* (2002) **29.** We Can Remember It For You Wholesale **30.** Horatio Nelson **31.** *The Little Mermaid* (1989) **32.** *Beethoven* (1992–2003) **33.** WHAT: The last refuge of awakened humanity, deep in the bowels of the earth/*The Matrix* (1999–2003) **34.** *Pirates of the Caribbean: The Curse of the Black Pearl* (2003) **35.** *The Green Mile* (1999) **36.** **D**ata **A**nalyzing **R**obot **Y**outh **L**ifeform/*D.A.R.Y.L.* (1985) **37.** *Eye of the Needle* (1981) **38.** Cook/Steven Seagal in *Under Siege* (1992) **39.** Parador/Richard Dreyfuss in *Moon Over Parador* (1988) **40.** *Shadowlands* (1993).

39 TOO DIFFICULT

1. Shelmikedmu/named after his three children, Shelly, Mike and Edmund (*Krippendorf's Tribe* (1998)) **2.** 555-HAIR/*Goodfellas* (1990) **3.** Lawrence Woolsey/John Goodman in *Matinee* (1993) **4.** Highway Patrolman **5.** An attractive guy/*Clueless* (1995) **6.** A phone booth/*Phone Booth* (2002) **7.** Jennifer/The names of the three hijacked oil rigs in *Ffolkes* (1980) **8.** For taping another kid's butt cheeks together/Emilio Estevez in *The Breakfast Club* (1985) **9.** 33/*Four Weddings and a Funeral* (1994) **10.** Karen Silkwood/Meryl Streep in *Silkwood* (1983) **11.** John Landis **12.** 19, 40, 4, 7, 25, 29 (in that order) – IEP 6,894,620.00/*Waking Ned*

(1998) **13.** Betty Sizemore/Renée Zellweger in *Nurse Betty* (2000) **14.**
Water/*Water* (1985) **15.** Tulip/Cirrus. Socrates. Particle. Decibel.
Hurricane. Dolphin. Tulip. – The seven key words used to imprint David in
A.I. – Artificial Intelligence (2001).

40 THE FINAL QUESTION
1. *The End* (1978).